Self-Publishing Success

- THE WORD -

Defined, Dedicated, Determined.

Ocean Reeve

Originally developed 2010

National Library of Australia Cataloguing-in-Publication entry

Author:	Reeve, Ocean (Author)
Title:	Self-Publishing Success; The Word – Defined, Dedicated, Determined / Ocean Reeve
ISBN:	9780992486808 (paperback)
Subject:	Self-publishing
	Electronic publishing
	Publishers and publishing
Dewey Number:	070.593

Published by Ocean Reeve.
www.oceanreeve.com

CONTENTS

DEDICATION

I dedicate this book to my wife. You have always believed in me. For that and many other things, I thank you.

ABOUT THE AUTHOR

O cean Reeve is a 39-year-old publishing executive. Since 2002, he has worked in key aspects of publishing within New Zealand and Australia. He has held roles such as the manager of a digital production and book distribution department, a sales representative for a traditional publishing house and an educational publishing house, a publishing consultant for independent authors, a sales & marketing manager and even the full management of a self-publishing company and staff.

Prior to this, Ocean held roles in other means of entertainment as Programme Director for Regional Television, Radio Host, Nightclub Promotions, and Director of an Online Video Marketing Business.

In 2010, Ocean was awarded the 'Kia Ora Mai Supreme Awesome Service Award of New Zealand' for his assistance in guiding authors through the self-publishing process and bringing their books to life. A year later, he relocated to Australia to continue his journey assisting thousands in their publishing journey.

Ocean is married with two children and two step-children and currently lives on the beautiful Gold Coast of Queensland, Australia.

INTRODUCTION

O ver the years in this industry, I have learnt a lot about what to do and what not to do when travelling the train that is publishing. I have worked for four different companies that all held their strengths and weaknesses when it came to bringing a book to life.

When the internet really started to show its power and influence early in the new millennium, we saw the fall of many traditional industries and the publishing world is one that took a massive hit. But there has been a shining light: self-publishing.

There are many good books on self-publishing and gurus who offer expertise in this industry and as much as I enjoyed reading them, I felt there were too many paths offered to the potential author where many of them lead to nowhere. I felt it was essential to produce a book that does what none in the past have done: it breaks down the most necessary and essential stages in publishing for all to know and access. Self-publishing is not just about writing a book and posting it online for all to absorb. You need to know the key areas in the process to ensure that you are giving you and your book the best possible chance of success.

I have learnt an immense amount through the experience I have gained; the people I have met and worked for over the years have helped me build up information and guidelines about working for the most important person in this entire industry: the author.

It is the author who lives with passion, writes for months, even years, and it is the author who should be enjoying and achieving their success. The rewards, whether financial, emotional, spiritual, or educational, are the authors' to enjoy. This book puts the author first and gives all the tools required to truly achieve the goals they set.

If you are writing fiction or non-fiction, this book guides you through each stage in chronological order. By the end of this publication, you will have the core essentials to confidently embark on your publishing journey. To a writer, self-publishing is an incredibly powerful and alluring concept. On the simplest level, it's an intriguing solution to an age old problem: How do you get your words to a wide audience? On an artistic level, it is a fantastic extension of the creative process. Beyond putting words on the page, the self-publisher actually controls every aspect and calls the shots, makes the final decision and with guidance from professionals and experts in their field, creates the physical and/or e-book and actively brings it to an audience.

The process can be broken into three major steps. The first step is to write the book and prepare it for editing. The second is to embark on the key pre-press steps to bring the book to a trade standard and a presentable look, feel, and print. The third is to market and promote the book on a local, national, and international level. Start marketing the minute you start writing by telling people that you are writing. It builds anticipation and pre-market appeal.

Ascertain your goal from the beginning. If your goal is to build a small business with your book or establish yourself as a fulltime author, there are some business procedures that you will need to embark on and some of these would be good recording and accounting steps for your smaller projects. As a self-publisher, you are operating a small business. Depending on where you live, starting a small business means jumping through a few hoops. For example, create a publishing name that nobody else is using. The name should include the word "publishing," the word "press," or the word "books." You will need to organise a business number or license. Check your country's guidelines to this process as it will differ from territory to territory. Also, look at getting a post office box, so you can receive mail relative to the project outside of your home address.

Create a bank account dedicated to your book project. Make sure you tie it to a PayPal account. You don't want to mix your business accounts in with your personal budget, so separate them right from the beginning. It also helps establish and clearly clarify profit margins, taxes, sales numbers, and more.

Technically when running a business, no matter how small, you will most likely be qualified for various tax benefits. For example, if you write in your home office, then part of your rent or mortgage payment can be a work deduction, as well as your computer equipment, book storage space, etc.

To get the full rundown of what you can and can't deduct, you'll need to talk to an accountant or business mentor. I am neither; I am a self-publishing authority that advises the most comprehensive and structured path to self-publishing in this new age, and I am about to outline this for you.

I mentioned earlier the many paths that other books offer. This book offers choices along the way, but also offers one correct method to bring a quality publication to life. This book will help you make it available for sale, and will advise you on how to market it successfully.

Mark this day in history because as you turn the next page, you begin the journey that many talk themselves out of. You are committing to an enjoyable, satisfying, and profitable journey that will be leaving your footprint on this earth, never to be lost or forgotten. Your legacy begins with the next part of this amazing process that brings your creative works to life.

THE WORD:

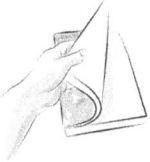

Start marketing from the minute you start writing. Build the anticipation.

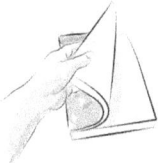

Ascertain your goal(s) from the beginning.

WHY SELF-PUBLISH?

Let's be honest, most writers' goals are to be picked up by a big time publisher and become the next J.K Rowling, Dan Brown, Stephen King, or even E.L James. Some of us even aspire to make writing our career and why not? Isn't one of our most common goals to do something we love as a job? I know that is mine. The reality is that the traditional way of publishing is just too hard to break into, unless you are an established and well-known individual or you are writing something of an extremely topical nature.

Ever since the introduction of the internet, social media and online publishing, the traditional publishing industry has been taking a standing 8-count. The question that stands now is how much longer do we give it before we are fully online? Until the publishing houses completely remodel their processes? Well, while we wait for the inevitable, the growth and successes of independent and self-published books and authors have been phenomenal. We are seeing regular successes both on a national and international level.

We are seeing self-published authors making it into the top ten international best sellers' lists. We are seeing independent writers being commissioned by magazines and publishers on and offline. We are seeing independently published eBooks revolutionise the industry. It can happen!

The goals mentioned above are even more credible today than ever. The opportunities for independent and self-published authors are much greater and more accessible because of the internet, and it goes without saying that from a promotional and marketing level, the worldwide web offers a worldwide audience at our fingertips.

Now, it is time to establish your goals and you need to physically write these down. By writing it down, you are manifesting the goal to be a reality, so go and grab three standard pieces of paper and a black permanent marker. We are going to write three main goals. One will be your initial goal, the closest to where you are at now. These will change as you begin the process and achieve each goal. By doing this, you are setting guidelines, timeframes, and expectations of yourself to actually follow through and achieve the second goal. Your initial goal approaches the steps along the way, so let's look at some examples:

- Finish writing the book by June.
- Have second draft for reader review by October.
- Lock down cover design procedure by November.
- Organise payment structure for printing.

As you can see, it will look much like a to-do list. Don't try and write down everything, just the ones that are your immediate focus. As I mentioned, these will change as they are achieved and with the right guidance from the experts, you will easily map out the others. On completion, you will end up with a bullet point procedure to bring your book to life. This will set the template for all future books.

I believe the second goal is two-part, and should be the same for every author regardless of your book's topic. We will call this the publishing goal:

- <u>Publish my work</u>: Defining the word 'publishing' is 'making public'. This has to be a set goal for all, even if it is a family history or your memoirs.
- <u>Ensure I make my investment back</u>: Self-publishing costs money, so you need to create a realistic and achievable financial forecast calculation sheet to show how this will be achieved. We will discuss how to do this later in the book.

Finally, set your BHAG (Big Hairy Audacious Goal). This could be any of the following and don't hold back; if it's something you wish to achieve with this book, put it down. Examples could be:

- Sell 1 million copies.
- Make 1 million dollars.
- Build a business from the profits.

Now that you have outlined your three areas of goal-setting, pin them by where you write and work on your project. They will stand as a reminder of what needs to be done and why you are doing it. It will keep the goals real and active and become a living and breathing entity that grows with you and your book.

Due to the developments in the publishing industry and growth in internet marketing, it has meant that one of the greatest changes in traditional publishing is the need for authors to do large amounts of marketing. There was a time when an author would write the story and once it had reached the publisher, the author would sit back and let the experts do their job, from editing and design, through to marketing and promotion. The author would receive their small percentage of royalties and rely on the publisher to do a marketing campaign that would sell millions.

The same deal applies today, but with the exception of the author's involvement in marketing and promotion being a large percentage of the campaign. Often this will be overly time-consuming, frustrating and a negative experience, especially if the author did not have the confidence to promote or make public appearances. Amongst all of this, the royalties remain the same. So to answer the question as to why should we self-publish - Why not? Doesn't it make more sense that you, as an author, should reap the benefits from the marketing and promotional efforts, considering you are required to do it anyway?

But this is just the latest reason as to why self-publishing has become a more popular choice. When I first entered this industry, I was surprised to see that authors had very little say in the editing, formatting, and cover design process.

This was left up to the publisher and often, when additions and deletions to the manuscript were challenged by the author, they were shut down immediately. To me, that seemed illogical. Shouldn't the person who has lived and breathed the story have a say? Shouldn't the writer who has expressed personal and emotional passion in their writing get consulted as to the look and feel their book will take? While the author needs guidance, assistance, and advice through the process of bringing their book to life, I believe that they need to have the absolute final say, even if it is to trust the judgement of the experts; it is the author who should be the decision maker.

Now let's talk about rights. As you all probably know, when signing with a publishing house, you are effectively signing the rights to your work away to the publisher. Not only is this the main basis as to why the publishers can decline author input in the process, but it is also a death sentence. In this new age of publishing, the life of a book is more limited than ever. Most books are discounted after 6-12 months and in some cases, even sooner. Once this happens, any remaining copies produced are discounted just so they are sold, which not only reduces the author's royalty, but also puts the title one foot in the grave. The author cannot revive the book as they no longer have the rights to do so. Let's say you wanted to release an eBook (if the publisher hasn't already), audio book or even submit the published work to a film producer. The bottom line is, you can't. This is the publisher's call and if they choose not to, then that's it. Game over.

So let's bullet these out because as you read through this ground-breaking new 'SELF-PUBLISHED' book, I want you to remind yourself that with independently publishing your own work, you will:

- Own the rights forever.
- Have input and final call on editorial and design.
- Receive far greater royalties from sales.
- Control the destiny and longevity of the story.

But, and there is always one, authors need the expertise that a publishing house offers. In the pre-publishing process of printing and marketing, it is important that the author is guided by people that are familiar and professional with this process and can be honest and advise them of the best course of action through every step.

Authors can't be expected to edit and proof their own work; they can't be expected to design a cover or bring the contents to a trade standard; they can't be expected to know the right process and prices involved in printing, and they can't be expected to market and promote the completed publication on their own. There are hundreds of companies that offer these services, but make sure you do your due diligence. If you can't physically meet with the company representatives, then request a Skype meeting. You need to feel confident that those you hire to assist in bringing your passion to the world understand you and your goals. You need to feel you can trust them and that there is transparency with the process, timeline, costs, and what they specifically will do for you and your publication.

Make sure you can clearly establish a long term and beneficial relationship. Be confident that the company you choose will do their best to bring your goals into reality and make sure you shop around. I recommend that you write your goals and services required in an email and request a quote and call back clearly stating that you wish to meet in person or via Skype. Copy and paste the email and send it to 5-10 companies and try and stay within your own country. My estimation is one, maybe two, will come back and specifically address your questions and be able to commit to a face to face. Don't settle for second best when self-publishing. If you truly want to reach those goals, then you need to stay committed to bringing the best out of your work and this includes the team of people you bring on board to help.

Over the years, I have seen some fantastic successes within the self-publishing industry from authors selling tens of thousands of copies, reaching best seller lists, and even being approached by publishing houses with offers. Whilst I always believe in never signing your rights away, if you are approached by a publisher after proving the book's success, then at least you will now have negotiating leverage. Whatever does happen, the most important factor with this journey is to enjoy it and make sure that the financial forecast calculation balances out (see more on this later). Enjoying the process of publishing and promoting should be as enjoyable as writing it and believe me when I tell you I have seen this happen in hundreds of cases. To me it is the author, the book, and the connection between the two that makes this journey truly wonderful and satisfying.

THE WORD:

Write down your goals, no matter how big, focusing on Initial, Publishing and BHAG, and make sure you post these by your work station or computer.

Self-publish for maximum royalties, author control, owning the rights and control destiny.

PLANNING FICTION

L et's start by dispelling the major myth that you have to be a talented writer to write a book. This is not the case at all. You don't need any major writing skill to write a book. If you can write an interesting letter and explain an event to someone, then you can write fiction, and the more you practise your writing, the better you will get. The techniques and processes in this chapter will allow you to go through the stages that can make writing a book a lot easier than you might think.

It is difficult for us to write a sequential book of stages that perfectly represents everyone's experience of the correct procedure for writing fiction. There are many types of fiction, so at times, the sequence that follows will be more or less relevant to the area in which you have decided to work. This is a guide only and offers a simple and effective process to create a flowing, fictional tale. We all build our own process when writing and how we approach it, but for a beginner, I strongly recommend mapping it out as follows.

When approaching the planning stage it helps to approach it using the Six Ps of fiction: Prepare, Plan, Plot, People, Places, and Premises.

Prepare

The first stage of writing a book is to thoroughly prepare. It can save you a lot of work later if you have clearly thought through the whole book before you start the actual writing. Let's highlight some sensible steps you may wish to start with.

The first major step is making the decision to write a book. If you'd like to, YOU CAN, and you can guarantee to have it published, so why not? Just make the decision!

Next, you need to make sure you can find time to write. Think about when you are at your best mentally and when you are least likely to get interrupted. It may only be for an hour a day, as long as it is a focused and comfortable time slot. Writing can be tiring as it does exercise your brain, and after a good session it may feel like you have just done a physical workout. Over time, you can increase the allowable time if it balances out. Make sure your workstation is comfortable and have reminders and motivators around to keep the eye on the prize. It is recommended that you actually write with a black marker on an A3 piece of paper what your goal for the book is. Then tape it in a clear viewing spot where you write. Whenever you are feeling blocked or demotivated, look up and remind yourself of why you are following your dream.

One of the most efficient marketing tools for any product or service is word of mouth, so tell everyone that you are writing! Build anticipation and excitement early on, as it will help with your first run of sales. We'll talk about this later.

Set milestones along the way when writing and reward yourself when you reach it. Write the milestones down as another motivational tool as the passion when writing exits by your own drive. When you achieve that milestone - savour the moment.

In the early stages of becoming a writer, think about staying within your comfort zone to a large extent. Write what you know. Take the time to write a list of things that you are interested in, moments you have experienced that others may benefit from knowing about, or that you would really like to learn about as you write.

Read a lot, especially in the genre that you are looking at writing. As we work through the various aspects of writing fiction, make a mental note to explore each in the book you are currently reading, and analyse how well that writer has handled these aspects of their writing.

Plan

Start to think about who your audience will be. Who exactly will want to read this book? Build the demographic. Age. Interests. Where are they? How easy are they to contact? Think of them as you write. Imagine that you will write the book as if you were writing directly for them and seeking to keep them interested and excited by what you write.

Think about what style, content, scenes, settings, activities, anecdotes, and people your audience would find interesting to read. Don't say the book is for everyone. If it is, it is too broad and you need to be more focussed on the specific interests of a specific audience.

Though not every author does this, it is wise to also think at this stage about the extent of the book – how many pages you expect to write. Once you know how many pages, you can estimate how many words and reward yourself with milestones. You can also set due dates for certain chapters or arcs. A good novel is usually in the range of 80,000-120,000 words.

If you're writing a children's picture book, the number of pages becomes quite critical to the costing, and for some binding options, you will need to write in multiples of four pages. Allow for the necessary introductory pages, such as the title page, imprint, and contents.

Knowing the size of the book you are writing helps to define the audience – a shorter fiction book is for a quick-read audience: commuters, magazine readers, or those who read for the topic (e.g. cowboy, erotic, romance, war stories). Long books tend to be for serious readers and suit explorations of deeper topics. Middle-length books suit crime, mystery, action – genres that attract readers of a range of abilities, so it's not necessary to spend a lot of time on development of depth. There are all the shades in between and plenty of exceptions to these few examples. You may sell more of a shorter book as the market is wider, but the price will be less. You may sell a lot fewer of a longer book, but you will call an excellent price as those who seek the last word on a topic are prepared to pay for it.

From this, think through what type of book you will write. Is it going to be written in the first or third person? Futuristic? Historical or current? Illustrated? If so, how? Free-flowing or academic in style? A tragedy, satire, comedy, drama etc.?

Think about the size of the printed book. When writing fiction, there are several options, but the most commonly used are these four: A-Format paperbacks are 110 mm x 178mm (4.33" x 7.01") in size, B-Format paperbacks are 130 mm x 198mm (5.12" x 7.8"), C-Format (trade paperbacks) is 135 mm x 216mm (5.32" x 8.51"), and A5 is 148mm x 210mm (5.83" x 8.27").

Plot

The next stage of planning involves developing the plot for the story. The plot is the core foundation upon which the entire work rests. By building this plot foundation carefully, the framework of the book will stand on a strong base and the book will come together more easily. A plot for fiction is the main storyline that runs through the work, and acts like the pencil sketch most artists do before they paint. It is well buried by the time the work is completed, but has acted as a strong guide which the painting (or in publishing terms; the book) is constructed.

Now that you have decided what sort of work you will write, it is time to work on your plot and on any additional narrative lines that will run through it to create interest for the reader. In a traditional episodic plot, the story progresses in chronological order from a beginning point from where the author begins to explain the story, through a middle where we often hit the height of the character arcs, and of course to an end point, the resolution of the character or story. It can also be the cliff-hanger, if you see yourself writing a series.

There are no rules as to how long a time period should be. In fiction, you can cover many generations or just a few hours; you might only cover a few minutes.

To develop a plot, you need to first realise that there is very little fiction that doesn't include a character or characters in difficulties at some point. There is no market for a story about nice people having a nice time. So you need to think about conflicts or problems that your character(s) might encounter.

A fun and successful way of highlighting possible problems and related action for a plot is to brainstorm for ideas. There are many ways to brainstorm. One way is to get a group of friends around and give each a pen and paper. Tell them some background to the type of book you are looking to write, then start with a topic such as 'problems a character fitting this genre might experience' and get them to write down anything they think of that relates to that topic. Verbalise the ideas. You can of course brainstorm on your own. Make sure you have a comfortable place to do it and some writers use music as an inspiration. Here's where we start calling our muse.

Repeat the brainstorming process as often as you like to develop various events, interactions, situations, and character moments, and once you have a strong list of ideas, sort them into groups of like ideas. Once you have found the core problems and events that will form the main plot, you can move on.

There is a range of ways to develop your plan, and these depend on the complexity of the writing you wish to produce. For a simpler piece of writing, use a large piece of paper or ideally a whiteboard, as you will most likely need to make changes as you go. Alternatively, cut yourself up some pieces of card. Lay out your plot in chronological order to allow you to see the beginning, middle, and end of the story. Remember, you want the beginning to be a strong enough idea to make the story come alive right from the start. Some writers, especially in a genre like murder mystery, prefer to start at the climax and work backwards to the beginning. Writers who choose this backwards approach find that it allows them to weave complexity and deception into the plot that make guessing the outcome much more difficult and enjoyable for the reader.

Often in fiction, there are sub-plots that follow along beside the main plot or weave through it in some way. These take different forms: red herrings, love interest, stories within the story, and twists and turns you didn't see coming. Think about what sub-plots you could attach to your main plot, and draw them into the plot's plan.

This is a good stage to start working more seriously on developing a working title for your book. This can be aided by using the friends brainstorming approach earlier mentioned. Tell them your target audience, style, and your storyline, and have them brainstorm possibilities. Work away until you find a title you feel you like and then grab it with both hands. Be excited about it. It is going to be with you for a while. Now, write a single sentence that you could use to tell someone what the book is about. Refine it until you have it in as few words as you can. Write this with your black maker and put it beside your goal. This will also help with focus and motivation.

People

Now it is time to work with the characters who will fill the pages of your book and perform the actions that make the story come alive. The characters in fiction are very important, as they are the central performers on the stage you have created. The quality and depth of your characters and the way you convey them are central to good fiction.

Your characters are real people and for them to come alive, it is important that they are contiguous in the mind of the writer. Without that, there will be a lack of integrity in the things they do, the way they are described, and the feelings they have. This will mean the audience will not relate to them and the whole story becomes a failure. Whether a character is an antagonist or protagonist or just a supporting player, the more alive they are to you, the more alive they will become as you write. One effective way to create strong characters is to develop their personal profile. Make a list of details about each main character, so that you really know them as people, and you will be able to construct their dialogue, actions, settings, thoughts, emotions, and choices. You should include their name, nickname, family, ethnicity, health and fitness, weight, height, occupation, qualities, moods, likes, dislikes, morals, hopes, dreams, fears, friends, partners, ex's, and children.

Once you have defined your characters, think about any mannerisms they are likely to have that may assist in distinguishing them, either through their dialogue or through their small actions (smoking, scratching).

You should now decide, if you haven't already done so, how the story is to be told; whose viewpoint will the reader see the action through? As writers, we need to supply the reader with a narrator, and often writers decide that this should be one or more of the characters in their story, though it is also quite valid to use a totally external observer – effectively the author. It is important to consider the best way to narrate your story for its genre. If one or more of the characters are to narrate the story, then every word they utter and every thought they have must be consistent with the character.

Narrating in the third person is probably the most common manner of telling a story; however, it leaves the readers to make their own judgements about the characters. It also allows the author to easily jump from one scene of activity to another without much explanation.

Keep research notes: Always carry a notebook as a tool for your on-going research. This is useful when defining your characters. Observe others and jot down any pieces of dialogue, actions, looks, etc., that could be useable for your characters.

Places

Next, it's the scenes in which you will set your story. These can have a great deal of influence on the vibrancy of the read, and a well-set scene is a great aid to readers and to their enjoyment.

Now that the characters and plot are established, you should be able to work out how many scenes you will have in your story.

A simple approach is to use coloured sticky dots to mark each scene change and, when a scene is revisited, use the same colour again.

Before finalising the nature of any scene, consider the capacity of a scene to assist in the building of character and impact. Also, look at the list of scenes you have created and mark any that have the potential to help define a character (e.g. a character's bed room) or help enhance the action (e.g. a love scene outside is always going to be more interesting to a reader than the same love scene in bed).

If there is any scene that is likely to be widely known, then there are easy ways to be able to describe the scene without actually having to go there and some simple research will fill in most of the details you need.

Premises

Next is the task of ensuring the merging into your plot of any symbolism, themes, or underpinning premises that you wish to convey. Sometimes these are overt symbols and sometimes more subtle, but by thinking them through with some care before you start writing, you can often sharpen thematic significance and keep yourself awake to possibilities once the words pour forth in the writing phase.

You have designed your characters, and this is the time to think what symbolizes the sort of person each is and the sort of journey they are on. What is each character searching for? It could be retaining or returning to the perfect world where everyone behaves themselves and justice is pure.

It could be safety and security for them and their child, or perhaps recognition for the quality of the work they do even though they are unconventional in the way they do it. You've probably read books with each of these underpinning premises.

Once you have decided what each character's motivations are, you can go back to your plot and character development and add anything that may be worthwhile to help carry that through.

Repeat this process with any enduring themes that you wish to merge into the book. These may be such things as 'you have to take the good with the bad', 'crime never pays', or 'love conquers all'.

Signposting is the art of making enough direction within the text so that the reader is comfortable about where you take them in your story and why. A story is killed if there is a big situation built up and then a totally unexpected character emerges from nowhere and solves it. You must have the reader happily accompany you, understanding at each point how a new place relates to the story, why it is necessary to go there, and how it relates to what's to come?

Remember that it's easy for you to know what you're thinking about, but the art of good writing is to convey this easily to the reader. You should set up signposts before any major event occurs. At this point, return to your plot and add any detail that is necessary to ensure that all characters, events, places, and key items that appear later on in the story are signposted in some way before they appear.

Finally, draw a line through your plot map to define the content of each chapter and then write a brief chapter outline for each.

Now you are ready to begin writing and your planning is clearly in place. The plot and character developments you have produced should always remain working documents able to grow and develop as you write.

THE WORD:

Prepare, Plan, Plot, People, Places, and Premises.

PLANNING NON-FICTION

When planning for non-fiction, the preparation to write is the same as it is with fiction. Comfort, time allocation, goal setting, milestones, and format are all important starting points and need to be addressed. Once you have established, you can begin the key parts of planning to write your non-fiction work. When writing non-fiction, you are calling yourself an expert in your field or offering accurate and accountable research and information.

Think about how you will collect your information. There is a wide range of popular non-fiction material on the market that is based on good reporting skills. To be a good reporter, you need the essential elements of good observation, interviewing, and researching skills. Personal experiences, unsolved murders and mysteries, shipwrecks and other disasters – if it is topical, interesting, amusing, important, then it can make a successful book in the report style.

Research is ideal for collecting content for certain types of publication. Research through the Internet can throw up all sorts of information and assembling this into a newly formed presentation is a useful and valid means of writing a book. Books have been published containing collections of recipes, collections on manufacturing instructions for commercial products, and all sorts of other things.

For more modern topics, researching from books is rarely ideal due to the rapidity of change, but for more historical content researching at your local library or museum can also provide the content for some very successful publications.

Diaries or logbooks often create an interesting, gradually unfolding look at an aspect of life and some famous tales have been told in this form. There are many situations that lend themselves to this sort of treatment.

Books can be produced as collections and email makes this process easier than ever. There have already been popular books produced by assembling the emails of two or more people into chronological order, as well as collections of humorous emails that pass around online, but the scope for this sort of approach is huge.

You can create an interesting book by either collecting a range of existing writings on a theme (be aware of copyright law) and present them as an edited anthology, or by asking a group of people to write on a related topic or theme and editing the collection.

Similar to editing is to collect all the various items in a range of written materials on the theme that you have chosen. For a shipwreck, for example, you might collect everything from the ship's loading list and the weather forecasts of the time, the logbook, letters of the mate, newspaper articles, photographs, and interviews.

For brief histories of schools, churches, or sports clubs, such collections are quite common and well enjoyed by those with an interest in that topic.

Make sure it is well researched to incorporate a wide range of material; collections can provide an amazing depth of understanding about aspects of interest related to a single entity, time, place, or event.

For those who are artistic, books of drawings offer opportunities. There are many books to be conceived that primarily use graphics for communication.

The web can be used as a research tool for seeking answers to specific questions, but it can also be used as a collection point for gathering a range of information on a wide range of topics suitable for publication. There are many ways to research online and many wonderful tools, such as Wikipedia and Google.

Just be aware that note-taking in these early stages could prove to be invaluable later – whether it's a rush of inspired thoughts or some factual material that supports your idea, a mind map showing the direction or exploration of a possible topic, or recording a book's details such as its title and author or a website URL, or an idea that a friend suggested.

Arrange

The next steps in planning involve developing the idea further by building up the foundation, then the framework. With writing, this is done through the processes of refining and focussing your idea by arranging and rearranging the sub-ideas you will put in your book.

Once again, we use a technique of brainstorming to develop lists of all the aspects that might be covered in such a book.

A simple and productive method at this point is to online brainstorm. Surf the web on the topic, choosing different search engines and see what comes up. Write down all the keywords or headings that are related to the general topic of your book, or that are related to the sub-topics you have. Don't worry about detail initially; we'll deal with that later. Just look for the broad scope of headings and subheadings that on the face of it seem relevant to the topic of your book.

Once you think you have exhausted your search for new headings, take your brainstormed list of ideas, and sort them into groups of ideas. You might need to first sort into one set of groups, then go back and sort each of those groups into further sets. This is an important stage.

You are now beginning the process of really refining and focussing the content of your book, based on the headings and subheadings you have formed. Looking at the topic and the lists you have formed, write a working title for the book, and then a single sentence that you could use to tell a person what your book is about. Do that now and refine it until you have it in as few words as possible.

Narrow

Now it is time to do some serious focus building, narrowing the ideas you have, shaping and re-shaping them to form the best platform you can on which to build.

First, define your audience. Who exactly will want to read this book? Where are these people? How do you contact them?

Out of a long list of possible questions related to audience, it will become clear that some are relevant to the type of book you want to write. Others won't be and as you discard them, it will help confirm in your own mind whether or not the topic and audience are a match. Look back to the extent, depth, and style headings you dealt with in the first section.

No matter what sort of book you are writing, it is important to keep it as focussed as possible. You have to keep it from wandering off-topic and becoming boring or laborious to gain information from. Cross out any of the listed topics or subtopics that can be left out without damaging the outcome you want for the group upon whom you are focussing. Ask yourself: is that section really appropriate to your working title?

Now that you effectively have the core topic headings and subheadings for your book, it is time to put these through the wringer too. Take each of the headings and ask the following questions: is it an appropriate heading for a book on this topic? Is it in the correct order in relation to all the other headings? Is it going to be followed by about the same amount of content as each of the other headings? Again, add, delete or edit headings and subheadings as you go through this process. Good planning and refinement at this stage will save you a lot of editing later, as it is very hard to reshuffle large amounts of information on a grand scale.

Check to see that that what you have is one book. You'll make more money with two or three books on a topic, each on a particular aspect, so be sure that you are still likely to stay within the planned extent, or divide the book into two or more.

Before you get too serious about breaking your book into pieces, make sure that your topic has enough content and structure for more than one book, without the risk of being repetitive.

Expand the single sentence you wrote earlier into a full framework. The framework should begin with the title and any subtitle, followed by half a page or so covering the scope of the book. This is an expansion of your single sentence, incorporating who your audience will be, how they can be located and marketed to, and any evidence you have found that indicates that they will buy the book. Write a chapter outline and expand each chapter with a paragraph or so explaining what will be covered as you work through your subheadings. It is important to feel convinced by this framework and that the book you are writing is of value to others. If you are not convinced, go back and look for the weak spots – it may be one particular chapter.

The blurb is the selling piece for the back cover of the book and is usually written with sales in mind. You need to know how to get the person who picks the book up to actually buy the book. You can always come back at the end and re-edit these pieces, but by having written them now, you have helped to clearly define the boundaries that the book will work within and the focus that it will carry. Make sure you write the blurb to appeal to your target audience, and edit it down to no more than 100 or so words.

Let's return now to your major headings. These should form the basis of your table of contents.

Tables of contents in non-fiction works quite often contain major section headings, then chapters or at least headed or unheaded subsections within those. So it is important to decide at this stage whether your major headings are to be section headings or chapter headings, and whether your subheadings are to be chapter headings, subsection headings, or just guiding topics you will use to write each paragraph or set of paragraphs.

You need also at this stage to consider whether the book needs an index. Remember that if the book is ever likely to be used as a serious reference book for research, it will almost certainly need an index. Creating an index, if your book warrants it, is another satisfying challenge to tick off. A great starting point for your index will be to capture the headings and subheadings you have already listed, which should probably be in your index. These can be linked straight away using an index tool to start your index list. Then, as you write the book, you can add any additional important ideas to your heading and subheading references in the index. By the end, you will have a well-referenced book.

What type of non-fiction book did you decide on? Some are more complex in their structure than others. As well as bibliographies and indexes, there can also be illustration credits, a glossary and appendices, endnotes, and so on. However, there is no need to be overwhelmed by this seemingly endless list of possibilities.

Be prepared and know that at the beginning of a book, there are a number of other pieces of information that you give the reader.

Even though you may not have paid much attention to these pages in the past, take a little time now to see what these are. You may need to write a short piece about yourself, list any previous publications on another page, and bear in mind that when you have finished writing the main text of your book, you are going to decide whether or not to include acknowledgements, a foreword, and a dedication. Front matter also contains the imprint page, which includes publisher and copyright details. When you're near to completion or finished writing, you will need to obtain from the National Library a 13-digit number, which is your ISBN number for this publication.

This number is your unique international standard book number and is used worldwide. You can get it earlier if you like; you can even get Cataloguing-in-Publication Data from the National Library to put on your copyright page, which gives cataloguers information on how to catalogue your book in their library. If an eBook is on the agenda, you will need more than one number. We take a look at this legal registration process later on.

Research

You should by now be feeling more focussed and beginning to move to the final planning areas before you write the text. Some of the work in this section will shape the text to make the writing fairly straightforward.

Now you have the shape of the book well-planned, it is time to get going on any remaining research. The most important research tool is the Internet and most non-fiction writers will want to become proficient in its use.

Specialist libraries and museums are perhaps the second most useful research tool, from the research rooms in your local library or museum, to specialist collections suited to historians, genealogists, researchers etc.

University libraries are extremely useful in this way and are usually open to all, though not for borrowing. A great deal of good quality research can be done in a library and if you can't take a laptop or ipad to record the research you find, then take photocopies or make notes and enter them later. Remember copyright and be careful not to include long passages from anyone else's work, and to reference any passages you do incorporate. Here again is where you show your efficiency and forward planning by remembering to write down all the details if you are intending to quote other people.

Work steadily through your headings and subheadings, collecting your information and storing it in a way that is useful and easily retrievable for you.

Keep a pen and paper always handy and use your phone as a recording device. It is surprising when ideas will come to you – often at the most inconvenient moments. You won't regret it.

As you research, you will want to build your bibliography. The best tools are libraries, universities, and of course, the internet. When formatting the bibliography, you should first list the author surname, then first names, the title of the work in italics, then the place of publication, the publisher's name, the edition if not a first edition, and the year of publication. Make sure you collect these details as you go along, as having to go back and find all of them at a later point is time-consuming

Returning once more to your headings and subheadings, it is time to think about paragraphs.

The better planned you are, the better you'll write. It is time to place a paragraph topic for each item that must be discussed under each subheading. This process will also clarify any more research you may need to complete.

Signposting is the art of making enough clear explanatory sentences within the text. Signposting in non-fiction can effectively mean beginning, middle, and end. To make the writing flow for the reader, each larger idea or subheading needs to be introduced, discussed, and then concluded as you move onto the next thing. Remember that it's easy for you to know what you're thinking about, but the art of good writing is never to leave your reader stranded. This means that you will normally have at least three paragraphs under any subheading: a beginning, middle, and an end to that section.

Once you have done your research, you are very close to being ready to start your writing. Create a timeline: a plan of what you wish to achieve each day and spread this over the time you have available to commit. This way you can progress at a steady pace and regularly reward yourself for goals achieved. Check at this time too, now that you have some idea of the volume of data you wish to incorporate in the book, that your work is likely to conform to the expected page allowance, and if it looks likely to blow out, you may like to rework some of the previous stages to tighten the scope of the work. Now, you are ready to write.

THE WORD:

Arrange, Narrow, Research.

WRITING FICTION

A t this point, you already know what type of story you are going to write and who your intended audience will be. You will have constructed a plot and designed a range of characters with a thorough character development. You will have divided your plot into scenes and planned how you will intertwine themes and core premises into the plot. You would have broken your story down to chapters so you'll know what is to be in each, and you will have done your research on any scenes and references, which need to be used in the story. You should have read plenty of material similar to the genre of book you want to write so that you have a feel for the style of writing you feel will fit the market.

About writing

The first thing to know about writing is that so long as you have the ability to put words together, such as to write an interesting email or text to a friend, then you have the potential to write a book. Perhaps the biggest block to good writing is that people tend to overcomplicate it, to try to sound like someone they're not, rather than just letting the words flow as they would if they were writing that email. So one of the best tips to good writing is to write first and worry about editing later. Let the words flow and find your own voice.

Keep a pen and paper beside you as you write. As you add detail, plot twists or new material, you will need to go back and check, add to or alter earlier sections, or amend the plot plan. Make a note to go back and change things later, so you don't lose the immediate flow of your writing and the sound of your own voice. Many of the most successful fiction authors have written using the template that less is more, but in a natural way. This makes the reader feel comfortable and means they don't have to work at reading it – it just fits, it's comfortable.

Quality beats quantity

Another essential key to good fiction is quality over quantity. When writing a book, write what needs to be said. You'll know, depending on who your audience is, just how much embellishment is expected. If you are writing for an arty, literary audience, they will expect to know the colour of the picture frame, the detail on the fire place mantle, and the brand of suit your lead character is wearing, because these are the sorts of things that they would notice themselves.

Audience

Think about your audience, and with an appropriate economy of words, tell all that a friend from that audience would want to know. You can always add more description or an explanation later if your early reviewers feel there is information missing. Your job as a writer though, is to make your audience feel that every word in the story is there for good reason.

If your review readers from your actual target audience confirm they find none of it boring or long winded, then you have done your job.

Pace yourself

Writing a book can be a long and sometimes laborious process. It may be the longest sustained commitment to a single complex task that many people achieve in their entire life and that is often part of the attraction many people have to becoming a published author.

There will be times where you find it hard to get motivated. This is the time to tell yourself that every great journey is accomplished by many small steps, taken one at a time. Recall the goal you wrote earlier and taped on the wall. Read the working title and the blurb again. Refresh yourself as to why you decided to write and don't set unrealistic milestones and targets for yourself. Take your time.

Feedback

One of the surest ways to lose motivation is to subject yourself to unhelpful criticism. Be careful who you let read your work in the early stages; protect yourself from that. There is plenty of time later for feedback at a time when you can more usefully use it and will indeed be seeking it to ensure you have written well for your audience. If it can't be helped and you decide to let someone go over your writing, be sure to let them know that you are just free-forming your writing at this stage. There is much more to be done.

If you do lose motivation to write at any point, just remember that a well-planned book does not even have to be written in chronological order. If you are stuck on a scene or find a part of the story to be tiring, take a break by going to another part of the story where there is a scene that you can picture well and that you feel ready to write about. It keeps the writing flow going.

Save

Always save your work. Ensure auto save is on for every 5 minutes or so. Keep a second copy on a USB and in a different place. Even email a copy of your work to yourself, that way if your computer crashes and you lose everything, you should still be able to access the latest file from any other computer.

Construction

Essentially, there is a beginning, middle, and an end, but within that work there is most certainly other beginnings, middles, and ends. In fact, each paragraph, each scene, each section, and each chapter also has its own beginning, middle and end. Whenever you are sitting down to write, whether it is a paragraph, a scene, or a chapter, think in these terms.

Paragraphs

Each paragraph should generally be related to a single idea. It should introduce that idea, expand it, and then in some way close it, which may lead into the next paragraph where a different point will be added.

These beginnings, middles, and ends need not be contained in separate sentences, but you should ideally see that the thought contained is complete. A paragraph could even be a single sentence. The following single-sentence paragraph might, for example, appear in the early stages of an action drama:

Within seconds of leaving the room, both he and Reece were blown to the floor with such intensity and rigor from the force of the C4 explosion, it felt as they were embedded into the floorboards.

You can see that it is a complete thought with a beginning, middle and end, though it may be quite tricky to define where one part stops and the next commences. In this instance, the commas are reasonable markers of the transition points between each.

Imagine you are driving across a desert road. The road is so long and straight that it disappears into the horizon and everything either side is sand. It might be fun to try for a while, but it would soon become fairly boring.

Now, just imagine that in the distance you spot something unusual, and as you turn you realise that it is taking you to somewhere quite different – an oasis. In a story, we need some of these turning points where a story suddenly takes a new and unexpected twist or a turn. Usually, a writer tries to make sure these are at the end of a chapter, as they entice a reader to keep going to see what happens next. When thinking about your chapter ending, think about turning points too and try to end as strongly as possible, ideally with a twist or revelation that will add depth and interest to the story. The endings of each chapter are almost as important as the ending of the story.

At the end of the story it is your call whether to bring the reader through to resolution or not. Some stories leave the reader hanging in that they don't get told whether the lead characters lived happily ever after. While it is common that readers are left hanging when there is likely to be a sequel, it is nonetheless an acceptable decision for the writer to make in any case. If you do go for resolution, make it strong. Many good stories are ruined by a weak final chapter that ties off every end and, in the effort to do so, sounds overly constructed. Famous authors generally end as strongly as they begin.

Types of writing

There are effectively three types of writing that can be used. They are descriptive, narrative, and dialogue, and the writer's art is to try to get a rhythmical balance between each. For example, a potted definition of each might be:

- Descriptive – verbal depiction of something or someone.
- Narrative – the act of telling a story or giving an account.
- Dialogue – the actual words characters utter.

Description

Be very careful of excessive use of adjectives and make sure you are aware of whose point of view you are writing from when describing a scene or another character. A great deal of descriptive information can be cleverly woven into the narrative and speech, such that one doesn't get the feeling of reading a description.

While there are times for extended descriptive passages, there are also means to eradicate them, so make the judgement – how will your audience prefer to receive the information?

Make sure that your text is alive with a richness of description that feels real; convey the sense that the author or character, whose point of view we are looking through, has actually been present and that this is a real place or happening. You, as an author, need to continually ask yourself questions about the setting, the person, or the activity. What is he wearing? What is on the table? What time of day is it? What can he hear?

Narration

The general rule is 'show me, don't tell me.' Keep the amount of narrative to a minimum and let the dialogue and descriptions of the scene carry the story as much as possible, while ensuring you are well aware of whose point of view is being conveyed in any narrative you do employ. The narrative can often be absorbed into good dialogue with interspersed description to achieve a smoother read, whilst still telling the story effectively.

Dialogue

When writing dialogue, try to make it sound as much like speech as you can, recognising that the written word will not be exactly the same as speech. Speech has very few full stops and frequently incomplete grammar, whereas written speech has to be sufficiently grammatical and well punctuated to be discernible to the reader.

In fiction, you often see spaces longer than a paragraph space left at the end of a paragraph. These usually signify scene changes and there can, of course, be a number of scene changes within a chapter, particularly where a work cuts between the present and the past, or between scenes of several different aspects of the story unfolding at once. Scene changes are progress markers and each needs its own beginning, middle, and end. A scene within a chapter may be just a glimpse of a larger unfolding scene, which we return to every now and then to observe progress, rather like someone flicking between options on a television set, but finding that each story has waited for you while you've been away.

Each smaller scene should contain as small a number of characters as possible. Sometimes the natural break points in a larger scene can be defined by additional characters arriving or when one or more characters leave a conversation or setting.

When writing a scene, the author should constantly be in the act of answering six key questions; *Who? Where? When? What? How?* and *Why?* These are answered primarily through the subtle use of dialogue, mixed with narration and description as necessary to adequately tell the story and describe features of the scene important to the nature of the work and the reader's experience with it.

Develop

Now it is time to break down your chapter plot planning firstly into scenes, and then into paragraphs. You can do this a chapter at a time just before you write.

Doing so gives you a chance to interplay the ideas from your plot in your mind once again before actually writing.

Your scenes should be largely self-defining – usually where there is a significant change in time, setting or characters – and it is quite possible and acceptable that your chapter is a single scene.

Once you have defined your scene, you need to write a few short sentences to define the key events that need to happen in that scene and how the scene adds to the overall gain in dramatic tension that you should be aiming to develop as your work unfolds. In effect, these are the descriptors for what each of your paragraphs in that scene will be about.

Once you have written the key sentences, check the beginning, middle, and end. Make sure the paragraphs you have planned are going to provide a strong opening to the scene that will once again hook readers to continue to read, then an effective and economic middle and a strong ending. Also review the description, narration, and dialogue for each paragraph. Plan first what can be conveyed in dialogue, then what still needs to be described or narrated. Remember to try to use as much dialogue as possible to tell the story and to convey descriptive ideas about things such as personality, mood and personal likes, dislikes, and strengths and weaknesses. Make a reminder to yourself to check which point of view the reader is to see through in each paragraph.

Take some time to see, hear, smell, and feel the setting your characters will be performing within the scene. What aspects of the characters do you wish to convey in the scene? In which paragraph will each be revealed and how? Remember to mix these up.

Make sure you understand what problems your characters face in the scene and why your characters will behave the way they will even though you may not necessarily reveal this to the reader at that point. If the motivations for such behaviour are to be revealed in any degree, what will be revealed, in which paragraph and how?

Consider again your characters' mannerisms – are they hard, gentle, loud, softly spoken, good, bad, or any part of these? Also, review if there are any symbols that could be used in this scene? Are there any opportunities to expand the core theme or the premise of the book and if so, where and how is this exposed?

Let the words flow

Let the words pour out quite freely onto the paper without worrying too much about reworking sentences or paragraphs to make them conform to the plan. Just get it down. Once you have written all the paragraphs of the scene, you can come back and rework each with reference to your planning; making sure that the flow is not damaged by your reworking. You should find that your story goes together smoothly and easily using this approach.

After you have written each day's work, read it aloud. Speak your dialogue out loud too. Only by putting it out in the air are you likely to be able to improve it to an extent that it sounds totally natural and free of the awkwardness that just wouldn't be present in normal conversation. Do a first edit straight after each day's writing, but leave the major edit to the end.

THE WORD:

Quality beats quantity. Know your audience and pace yourself, define your style and 'SAVE YOUR WORK'.

WRITING NON-FICTION

At times, a non-fiction work is a collaboration between a number of individuals. This approach is often employed for the writing of local or family histories. Effective planning includes laying down comprehensive guidelines. What can happen otherwise is that the input from various contributors can become very unbalanced and difficult to edit. Be aware that, right from the start, good planning and direction to contributors, including a writing plan, can save a lot of problems later. Some of the information in this chapter has featured previously in Writing Fiction so if you feel a little repetition coming through it is because the same message exists in both forms of writing.

The second point worth noting in terms of any sort of collaboration is that there are some tools to make version control very easy. For example, Microsoft Word has *Track Changes*, found under the *Tools* menu. Under *Track Changes*, you can send a person the manuscript, and they can make their alterations and additions under *Track Changes* and send it back to you. What you receive is their changes all marked in colour, with anything they deleted out to the side in a box. You can then review and either *Accept or Reject Changes*. It is a worthwhile tool and very useful when you send your finished manuscript to readers as part of the editing process. They can mark up their suggested changes straight in your manuscript and you can then accept or reject them. This is especially useful if there are more than just a few minor changes to a manuscript.

Another tool Microsoft Word has is called *Compare and Merge Documents* and is also found on the *Tools* menu. If you decide to send copies of your manuscript to several people, let's say three, and have them each send back their *Track Changes* alterations. You might accept the changes they each made, but now you have three manuscripts in addition to your original and each one containing differences. Using *Compare and Merge Documents,* you can bring each of the three up one at a time alongside your original one and have the computer show you the differences in the two. By accepting and rejecting as you wish, you can bring in all the changes. Again, a little experience in its use will make it seem like the simplest of tools.

Pace yourself

The following points we have covered in the Writing Fiction chapter but as it is applicable to this chapter as well, it is important that we state it again, plus you may have just come to this chapter skipping the fiction chapters.

Writing a book can be a long and sometimes laborious process. It may be the longest sustained commitment to a single complex task that many people achieve in their entire life, and that is often part of the attraction many people have to becoming a published author.

There will be times where you find it hard to get motivated. This is the time to tell yourself that every great journey is accomplished by many small steps, taken one at a time. Recall the goal you wrote earlier and taped on the wall.

Read the working title and the blurb again. Refresh yourself as to why you decided to write and don't set unrealistic milestones and targets for yourself. Take your time.

Feedback

One of the surest ways to lose motivation is to subject yourself to unhelpful criticism. Be careful who you let read your work in the early stages to protect yourself from that. There is plenty of time later for feedback at a time when you can more usefully use it and will indeed be seeking it to ensure you have written well for your audience. If it can't be helped and you decide to let someone go over your writing, be sure to let them know that you are just free-forming your writing at this stage. There is much more to be done.

If you do lose motivation to write at any point, just remember that a well-planned book does not even have to be written in chronological order. If you are stuck on a scene or find a part of the story to be tired, take a break by going to another part of the story where there is a scene that you can picture well and that you feel ready to write about. It keeps the writing flow going.

Save

Always save your work. Ensure auto save is on for every 5 minutes or so. Keep a second copy on USB and in a different place. Even email a copy of your work to date to yourself, that way if your computer crashes and you lose everything, you should still be able to access the latest file from any other computer.

Construction

Essentially, there is a beginning, a middle and an end, but within that work there is most certainly other beginnings, middles and ends. In fact each paragraph, each scene, each section, each chapter also has its own beginning, middle and end. Whenever you are sitting down to write, whether it is a paragraph, a scene or a chapter that you are thinking in these terms.

Paragraphs

Each paragraph should generally be related to a single idea. It should introduce that idea, expand it, and then in some way close it, which may be to lead into the next paragraph where a different point will be added. These beginnings, middles, and ends need not be contained in separate sentences, but you should ideally see that the thought contained is complete. A paragraph could even be a single sentence.

You can see that it is a complete thought with a beginning, middle and end, though it may be quite tricky to define where one part stops and the next commences. In this instance, the commas are reasonable markers of the transition points between each.

Whenever you are writing non-fiction, you must keep in mind who the book is speaking to and ensure the appropriate tone is adopted in the writing to appeal to that target audience. There is no point in writing in heavy academic terms if the projected audience is not academic.

Equally, you should not adopt too light and familiar a tone if you are seeking to capture the real interest of the serious technical reader. Try at all times to keep a typical projected reader in mind so that you retain the correct tone for the work.

Types of writing

There are effectively three types of writing that can be used. They are descriptive, narrative and dialogue, and the writer's art is to try to get a rhythmical balance between each. For example, a potted definition of each might be:

• Descriptive – verbal depiction of something or someone.

• Narrative – the act of telling a story or giving an account.

• Dialogue – the actual words characters utter.

Description

Be very careful of excessive use of adjectives and make sure you are aware of whose point of view you are writing from when describing a scene or another character. A great deal of descriptive information can be cleverly woven into the narrative and speech, such that one doesn't get the feeling of reading a description.

While there are times for extended descriptive passages, there are means to eradicate them, so make the judgement – how will your audience prefer to receive the information?

Make sure that your text is alive with a richness of description that feels real; convey the sense that the author or character, whose point of view we are looking through, has actually been present and that this is a real place or happening. You, as an author, need to continually ask yourself questions about the setting, the person or the activity. What is he wearing? What is on the table? What time of day is it? What can he hear?

Narration

The general rule is 'show, don't tell.' Unlike with fiction where I encourage you to keep the amount of narrative to a minimum and let the dialogue and descriptions of the scene carry the story as much as possible, with non-fiction it is more the opposite where the narrative can often be the key story telling method. However, ensure you are well aware of whose point of view is being conveyed in any narrative you do employ. The narrative can often be absorbed into good dialogue with interspersed description to achieve a smoother read, whilst still telling the story effectively.

Dialogue

When writing dialogue, try to make it sound as much like speech as you can, recognising that the written word won't be exactly the same as speech. Speech has very few full stops and frequently incomplete grammar, whereas written speech has to be sufficiently grammatical and well punctuated to be discernible to the reader.

As with fiction, with non-fiction you often see spaces longer than a paragraph space left within a paragraph.

These usually signify scene changes and there can, of course, be a number of scene changes within a chapter, particularly where a work cuts between the present and the past, or between scenes of several different aspects of the story unfolding at once. Scene changes are progress markers and each needs its own beginning, middle, and end. A scene within a chapter may be just a glimpse of a larger unfolding scene which we return to every now and then to observe progress, rather like someone flicking between options on a television set, but finding that each story has waited for you while you've been away.

Each smaller scene should contain as small a number of characters as possible. Sometimes the natural break points in a larger scene can be defined by additional characters arriving or when one or more characters leave a conversation or setting.

When writing a scene, the author should constantly be in the act of answering six key questions: *Who? Where? When? What? How?* and *Why?* These are answered primarily through the subtle use of dialogue, mixed with narration and description as necessary to adequately tell the story and describe features of the scene important to the nature of the work and the reader's experience with it.

Anecdotes

It has been shown time and time again that one of the most effective means of making a non-fiction book more readable is to include plenty of stories within the text. These lighten up the reading and can be used very effectively to illustrate points, or in fact to tell part of a story. It is quite acceptable to differentiate anecdotes and stories from the general text of the non-fiction work in various ways.

Sections

In non-fiction, as in fiction, we usually signify sections within a chapter by leaving a larger space between paragraphs. Your sections should be largely self-defining.

Section breaks usually occur where there is a significant change of topic or focus within the overall topic of the book, but not so significant as to make it another chapter.

In a book, for example, on America's top fifty companies of all time, you may define your chapters based on districts from which those businesses arose, and your section breaks within introduce each new business to be discussed. Alternatively, you may make each of your chapters based on periods at which the top fifty businesses were started (e.g.1840–1860, 1860–1880, 1880–1900, etc.) and use the section breaks within each chapter to mark the different businesses that were started within that era.

You may even choose to make the book fifty chapters long and to discuss each business one at a time, with section breaks marking where you start to discuss each new era of each company's development.

As you can see, there are no hard and fast rules, it is simply one way of structuring your content to gain the best presentation, and you don't have to have any sections at all. But, as you can also see, there is a great deal of potential to make a book containing the same basic core of information more or less interesting, depending on the way in which you present it.

Final plan

Once you have defined your paragraphs and sections, write a few short sentences to define the key points that need to be covered in each section. In effect, become the brief descriptors for your paragraphs. Once you have written the beginning, middle, and end, are the paragraphs going to provide a strong opening that will hook readers to continue reading? Is there an effective and economic middle, and a strong ending? Also, review the description, narration, dialogue, anecdote etc. For each paragraph, plan the approach by which the information can best be conveyed in an interesting and informative manner appropriate to the type of work.

Photographs

Choose photographs with good definition if you are printing in black and white. If you have older photographs or newer ones of a generally dark nature, you will need to look at the possibility of having these lightened in the design process. All photographs will need to be supplied at a high resolution (at least 300dpi) in a JPEG or TIF format.

Index

The task of creating an index used to be an exacting and arduous one, but today, with the assistance of your computer tools, it can be achieved much more simply.

As you write, keep a note of terms, headings and subheadings that you feel ought to be included in an index of the book.

Normally these include the names of key people, places, things, and events. We suggest you open a second document that sits on your task bar as you write. As you write about anything that should be included in the index, add the reference word to the index document. Then you can refer back to this when you start to create your index in your manuscript.

Once the book is complete and properly edited, so that you are sure you won't have to make any more changes, take each word on your indexing list in turn and in your manuscript document, using the *Find* facility under the *Edit* menu, mark each as an index entry.

Follow-up

After you have written each day's work, read it aloud. By voicing it, you are far more likely to hear and see errors that you may miss if you just scan the work in silence.

Leave your work for at least a week after that and then read it once more, looking not just for spelling errors but also for grammatical and structural faults as repetitiveness, poor sequencing, inadequate explanations or arguments, style changes, paragraphs or ideas that seem to be out of order or that could be better arranged, contradictions and so on. Work it to an extent that it sounds totally natural and free of awkwardness, and then leave the major edit to the end.

THE WORD:

Pace yourself and define your structure.

'SAVE YOUR WORK'.

LEGAL MATTERS

There are legalities involved in almost everything we do and it is no different when publishing a book. Please note, that while I have sound knowledge in this area, I am not a lawyer and if the following chapter raises any areas of concern, I recommend seeking legal advice so you know where you stand.

Once you've created something original, you want to ensure, whether it is published or unpublished, that it is protected. It's easy to do, and there are two ways that this can be approached.

Auto Protection

Make sure you have investigated the law for your area. In most countries, we have the Protection of Literary and Artistic Works, which ensures that your work is protected from the moment you create it, as long as it was created with the aid of a machine or device. In other words, as long as it is in a readable form. To see if your country is listed with these rights, visit the World Intellectual Property Organization (WIPO) at http://www.wipo.int/members.

Fix the date of your copyright. This will protect you should there ever be a legal ownership dispute in the future.

There are several informal ways to do this without officially registering the manuscript, though there is no actual provision in copyright law regarding these methods.

The most obvious method of fixing the date of your copyright is by viewing the date it was created on your computer. This is recorded from the very first word written and can always be regarded as an accurate record of copyright. You can also mail yourself a copy of the manuscript, and the postmark will be evidence of the date of copyright. Don't open it once you've sent it, or it will mean nothing.

By showing your work to friends and family, you will have witnesses to call on should you ever need to verify the date of your copyright.

As I mentioned earlier, the law in most countries states that you own the copyright of the work as soon as it is fixed in a readable format. By placing the copyright symbol (©) on your work, you are telling others that you know your rights. Again, secure a legally-relevant date of original creation. For example, write '© 2013' and add your name. Follow it up with the standard copyright statement: *No part of this publication may be reproduced, stored in a retrieval system or transmitted in any form or by any means without the prior written permission of the author.*

Pseudonyms and Pen Names

Writing under pseudonyms is nothing out of the ordinary, many do it and for various reasons. So whether it is to keep your identity secret, to have a name more agreeable to your desired market (i.e. Dr Seuss for children's books) or a general marketing tool, whatever name you publish under, you still automatically own the copyright to your own book just by having written it.

However, if you are ever faced with a scenario where you need to produce proof of ownership over your work, in a copyright infringement case for example, does having a pseudonym become problematic?

Copyright registration requires certain information about the author and the owner, and this information is a matter of public record. But an author publishing under a pseudonym for any of these reasons may not have a need for complete security, especially pen names used by children's authors.

The copyright procedure makes it easy for an author to provide a pseudonym in conjunction with their legal name and from this the copyright certificate is all the official evidence the courts might need to show the author's connection to both pseudonym and intellectual property.

As I mentioned earlier, authors may have very different reasons for using pseudonyms, reasons that do require publication to take place in absolute secrecy. For example, the material could have strong political impact and a pen name could be used to prevent any government retaliation, especially in less democratic countries. Another reason, one I am very familiar with, is to keep the author safe from retaliation by the public due to their book being of a controversial nature. I recently have been involved in the publishing of a book that attacks the child safety department in Australia.

It revolves around a woman's battle to hold onto custody of her son during a very bitter and violent separation dispute. She felt to protect herself, but still get her story out there, she needed to write under a pen name.

In these types of situations, creating a public record connecting the author's real name to the work could become very problematic. It's perfectly legal for an author to register their copyright under a pen name without revealing their true identity, but what happens when there is a requirement to prove legal ownership and the author's legal name doesn't appear on the copyright registration?

Copyright law can become quite a complex issue but there are a number of ways to prove the connection with a pen name, but they are external to the copyright procedure itself. In these cases, it's important to speak to a lawyer about preparing the necessary paperwork that connects your name to your pseudonym so that your connection to your pseudonym is legal and undeniable.

Official Registration

Registering your copyright in your own country is generally a straightforward process and can usually be done online. Some countries, such as the United States, offer the ability to officially register a work for copyright. Other countries, such as Australia or the UK, have no method in place for official registration of copyright. Copyright does not protect ideas. It only protects works, so you need to write your ideas into tangible form.

ISBN, CiP and Legal Deposits

The International Standard Book Number (ISBN) is a 13-digit number that will uniquely identify your book internationally. While an ISBN is not mandatory, and does not provide copyright on a work, it is the principal world-wide ordering signature for the book trade and library market. Your barcode that features on the back cover is created from this number. International Standard Book Numbers are available through your own country's representative, whether it be the National Library, Ministries of Culture, Nielsen Book Services or similar. When registering for an ISBN for your title, you can request one number, a block of ten, or even 100. It is recommended to get a block of ten as you will need a unique number for your eBook and of course once you have achieved success with your first book, you may want to write another.

Cataloguing in Publication (CiP) is the data prepared in advance that catalogues the publication by the national library of the country where the work is to be published (or the country's equivalent). The name reflects the usual practice of including that information in the publication. Each national library maintains a database of the entries it writes, which includes the library's Dewey Number record.

Most countries also have a legal deposit process where once the book is officially ready to be released, you are required to send copies to the National and even State or Provincial Libraries. The amount of copies required can vary from country to country, but this will be explained to you during the ISBN and CiP process.

Public Domain and Fair Use

I get asked the following question a lot; 'If I have used a quote, image or passage from someone else, do I need permission?' The quick answer is yes and if you fail to do so, technically this is copyright infringement. Reproducing someone's copyrighted work without their permission, even if you give them acknowledgement, is infringement. So be vigilant and seek the permission you need. In some cases, when you fail to hear back from the author or publisher and you feel you need to proceed, you may be able to fall back on the fact you have made every reasonable attempt to seek permission and as long as you can prove this, then liability may be reduced. But this does not clear you from the infringement as technically, not being able to contact the copyright holder is not entirely excusable. However there are two scenarios where this may not be an issue and that is if the material falls into one of the following categories; 'Public domain' and 'Fair Use'.

Public domain material refers to items that cannot be copyrighted such as an idea, title or name. It also includes material where the copyright has expired and/or has not been renewed. Most government documents and publications also fit under the public domain umbrella.

You also will not require permission if your use of the material qualifies as 'fair use' under the Copyright Act. In general, 'fair use' refers to a short excerpt used in connection with genuine criticism, parody, or teaching. Use of material in a review or educational article is 'fair use' however use in novels is not. For example, including lyrics from Bruce Springsteen in your novel is not 'fair use'.

Seeking Permission

Gaining permission should be relatively easy and depending on the context of the material, you may easily gain a positive response. Traditional publishers cause the biggest blocks for such requests as they aim to ascertain what they can make out of it. Recently I had an author wishing to use a quote from J.R.R Tolkien's 'The Lord of the Rings' in his book. He had made contact with the Tolkien Estate who acknowledged receipt of his request and informed him they would let him know. Following months of waiting and regular follow up emails all to no avail; it reached the point where the author just wanted to go to print. He asked my opinion on whether he should include the passage and I instantly replied with an affirming 'NO!' Don't risk it, it is not worth it and can be the undoing of such a positive process and experience. Obviously the author needed to decide how important to the main body of work the quote was and if there needed to be any revision so that it would work without it. He followed my advice and removed the passage.

How do you find the copyright owner? Generally this information will be featured on the imprint/copyright page of the publication. Publishers are easier to track down than authors, and could either manage the request themselves or in some cases, even put you in touch with the author. Libraries have many directories available, such as the Literary Marketplace, to help you find publisher's names and addresses. The Copyright Office in your country or alternatively, the National Library can also have this information listed in their databases; however that may incur a fee.

Based on Real People

When you write about real people you are exposing yourself to possible legal liability, even if you tell the truth. Simply changing the names is no solution because if the person can be identified by circumstances, appearance, or setting then you still have an issue. Disclaimers can help, but you shouldn't rely on them. To give a clearer picture, let's take a look at both defamation and privacy.

Defamation is when something has been written or said that negatively affects the reputation of a living person or organization. Looking back to the example I used earlier where an author using a pseudonym wrote negatively about the child welfare department, could they consider this defamation? As it is generally considered to be exposure to hatred, contempt, ridicule, or financial loss, then yes, it probably is. Libel is the written act of defamation and slander is the spoken act. Either or, the defamation must be communicated to someone other than the subject of the defamation. But remember, truth IS an absolute defence to this, so if what you have written is true and you can prove it, then it cannot be defamatory. Another defence to defamation is proving that what you have written is an opinion and not a fact.

Privacy law does have a clause in it relative to authors, two in fact, public disclosure of private facts, and 'false light.' Public disclosure of private facts occurs when a writer discloses private and possibly embarrassing facts about someone and it has no public involvement or concern. These can include publishing information about someone's sexual problems, physical, or mental ailments.

For example, publicising the fact that your neighbour has failed to pay her rent for three months, although true, would be an invasion of her privacy. However, this does not apply if the information published has come from sources of public record. Public figures have less of a right to privacy because of the public's legitimate interest in their affairs. For example, a magazine may publish a profile of a musician without fear of being held liable for defamation.

The other clause connected to the privacy law that applies to authors is 'False Light' and this can occur when some facts about a person that creates a deliberately false and misleading impression are published, such as when a newspaper publishes a story about criminals in jail and includes the name or photograph of an innocent person.

While this would not be considered a very enjoyable part of the publishing process, it is a vital one. I do not claim to be a lawyer and strongly recommend that you seek legal advice if these or any other issues are of concern. It may be the case of a simple phone call putting your mind at rest, but it also could be that same call saves you a whole lot of worry and stress.

THE WORD:

Always seek permissions.

Copyright ©

Legalities do matter. Always review your legal issues.

MANUSCRIPT APPRAISALS

Once your manuscript is complete, you have a choice to make. If your book is for the general market do you need a manuscript appraisal? Let's start of by explaining exactly what this is. A Manuscript Appraisal is a systematic and objective study of the marketability of your book, as well as an assessment of the revisions needed to ensure that the book is of the highest quality. Successful books almost inevitably have gone through revisions based on a Manuscript Appraisal, which is to be expected. Ultimately it is one of the earlier processes a serious author needs to undertake to ensure they have told the best possible story and to have the confidence that there is a market for their book. When you receive your appraisal back it should be giving you feedback on your title, length of book, desired format, pricing, subject matter and its potential popularity, author's expertise, competition, audience, marketing strategy if applicable, originality, focus, clarity, structure, validity, writing style, any plagiarism, suggestions for added value. It will be comprehensive and honest and will most definitely mean revising the book to ensure you are giving your book the best possible chance of success.

So let's take a look at who needs an appraisal. If you are writing a family history, autobiography or poetry you would not need one. These genres don't need such detailed analysis.

In some cases mind/body/spirit, general history, biographical and training manuals should get an appraisal, especially if the goal is to market globally. If you are writing self-help, educational, medical or business non-fiction that you intend to release on an international level then I strongly recommend you action the appraisal system. With fiction my response is an unwavering yes! Any book you are publishing that you hold high hopes and intentions on and planning to release globally should have an appraisal. Fundamentally it is to improve your chances of achieving your BHAG (Big Hairy Audacious Goal). Not only because you have ensured the manuscript has been bought up to the best possible standard but also because it will give you the confidence that you have an excellent product.

While you are familiar with the contents of your book you may not be as knowledgeable about the publishing industry, or about the market for books like yours. The appraisal process helps you tailor your book so it fits well with the needs of the audience for your genre and subject. This process gives you objective feedback from a professional who is new to your manuscript. As the author you have most likely worked on the book for months, maybe even years. This makes it impossible for you to step outside and look in at the book from a consumer's point of view. An impartial reading by a professional appraiser will reveal flaws in structure, style and content that you may have missed, identify mistakes and suggest alternative approaches so you can make the necessary revisions to your manuscript.

There is much debate about this. Many feel it should be done following the editing process but I feel that can be redundant, specifically for self-published authors as why would you pay for editing only to have an appraisal tell you it needs rewriting? I feel the ideal time to do an appraisal is when you feel that your manuscript is ready for a professional editor. In the next chapter I cover the process of preparing your book for editors and proof-readers. Once you have done this, prior to sending it out, action the appraisal. If your appraisal is favourable and you make adjustments that have been recommended then your editor and proof-reader will have a much easier job which ultimately should be quicker and even more economic. After all, most self-publishers are not millionaires and can't be expected to spend in an unstructured fashion. They need to know that once it passes a stage successfully it is ready for the next, going backwards is not really sensible.

So what can you expect to pay for this service? Well, it's not cheap and it shouldn't be. It is a very important and well-constructed process that is devised for you to succeed. However, what I find annoying is the variation of prices in the marketplace. For the sake of this explanation, and future ones throughout this book, when I quote financials I am looking at Australian dollars. If you are in the US remove 10%, if you are in New Zealand add 10% and if you are looking at the UK, double it and this should give you a fair comparison taking into account the fluctuating exchange rate. When researching for this book I found one place offering manuscript appraisals for $300. So whether your book is a 20,000 word short story or a 500,000 War and Peace epic, you will be charged $300? I don't think so. The true cost of an appraisal is worked out taking into account several factors; word count, genre, and any desired goals from the author. Here's an example; if you have written a novel of 80,000 words and aim for a national market then a likely fee for the appraisal will be anywhere between $400 –

600, however changing your goal to be international will likely show in cost as the research from the appraiser which could mean $600 – 800. My advice is to shop around; an appraiser should have a record of work and be able to clearly define their approach so you can feel confident you have chosen the right person.

One final piece before I close of this chapter – manuscript appraisals have developed over the years. Initially seen as primarily about content, nowadays with such large amounts of competition and online publishing and selling channels, it now includes marketing potential and your competition analysis. Be sure that this is included when choosing your appraiser. Value for every dollar spent is one of the key messages behind self-publishing success.

THE WORD:

If you're serious about success then an appraisal is needed.

Shop around. Ensure you find an experienced appraiser who has a track record

EDITING AND PROOFREADING

The process of taking a raw manuscript and bringing it up to a trade standard can be quite expensive if you haven't reduced the amount that the editor and the proof-reader has to do, so the cleaner you can get your own manuscript, the better.

Once you have completed your manuscript, the first step is to request that a group of well-selected friends, colleagues, and a selection of people within your target audience read through the manuscript and make suggestions for improvement. Social writers groups are excellent for this purpose.

The most commonly used software to write one's book is Microsoft Word, so we will focus parts of this section on its use for the purpose of preparing your manuscript for the editing stage. One of the best features of Word is that it contains several, very useful tools that make the process of receiving and assessing your edited manuscript simple.

The first feature is called *Track Changes,* found under the *Tools* menu. You click on this feature to turn it on, and when a person receives your manuscript, they make their alterations with *Track Changes* on and send it back to you. What you receive are their changes all marked in colour and/or sidebar comments, including formatting changes, deletions and additions. You then use *Accept and Reject Changes* to accept or reject each change or suggestion.

The second tool is called *Compare and Merge Documents* and is also found on the *Tools* menu. As I mentioned in the previous chapter, you might choose to send copies of your manuscript to several people - let's say three for the purpose of this explanation - and have them each send back their *Track Changes* document. You might accept the changes they each made on each of their versions, but now you have an additional three manuscripts along with your original and each one different from the next. Using *Compare and Merge Documents,* you can bring the manuscripts alongside your original, one at a time, and have the computer show you the differences in the two. You can then accept or reject the changes as you wish. The feature can also be used if one of your three readers fails to use *Track Changes* and just makes their edits straight in the document.

Make sure you have backed up your original manuscript onto a USB before beginning this process and as each *Track Changes* document comes in, save these also. Ensure your system for backing up the work is thorough as there is nothing worse than a computer crash that loses everything.

Even emailing versions through to yourself so you always have an e-copy backup is recommended. It is good practice not to delete any version, but to name the file with the date e.g. Vampire Wish 12.02.13, Vampire Wish 2.03.13, Vampire Wish 15.03.13. Keep all files until the book is completed, as it is very easy to accidentally lose parts of a book without realising or a file can corrupt. When the book is complete and in the production stage, save your entire folder onto a USB stick.

Grammar and Spell Check

Under the Tools menu in Word is the *Spelling and Grammar* check. You can use it as you write your manuscript to help you check your work, but as I suggested earlier, it is best done when the manuscript is completed. If you do add more text after your spell check, those pieces should also be checked. Getting the spelling correct is extremely important. The spell check will also give you suggestions when it picks up inconsistencies in the sentence structure and grammar usage.

Don't think your manuscript will be completely free of any errors though. A careful proofread is still needed by someone with expertise in this area.

There are really three parts to editing. They are structural editing, copy editing, and proofreading. In many cases, two or more of them will be done simultaneously or by the same person, but it is nonetheless handy to understand the purpose of each so that you can ensure that each is done well enough to make your work a high quality, professionally finished product.

Structural editing

Once your reader's documents come back to you and if you're feeling from the comments and your own thoughts that the book needs improving to be of a trade standard, then it is recommended to contract a structural editor. A structural editor's role involves ensuring that books are readable and easily comprehended, tightly written and economical with words. A structural editor will eradicate poor sentence structure, sudden leaps of tense, weak scenes, characters or events, general pillowing and carry on with the basic proofreading tasks.

A well-edited book is a pleasure to read and rarely difficult to follow. A good structural editor should ideally also be a good writer, able to retain the unique 'voice' of the particular author whose work they are editing, whilst ensuring that the correct structure of the story or manuscript is complete.

Because authors tend to write over a period of time, they can often miss inconsistencies, such as the colour of their lead character's car, names, and specific character traits which may have changed as the manuscript developed. Some structural editors like to create detailed notes of the characters, places, times and events as they read, so that any inconsistency is easily highlighted.

For all authors, their work becomes a part of them and it can often seem like a massive hit when people criticise it. The roles of editors and publishing staff demand that criticism is offered and accepted. It is part of the necessary tasks in this process to make your book the best it can be.

There are several online websites with listings of editors available for work and this is the most logical place to start - but try to keep it local. Stay within your country. Websites that are linked to a Society of Authors in your region would be the first logical choice, but if you choose to go wider, websites such as guru.com, elance.com, and oDesk.com have profiles advertising a large number of qualified and experienced editors. But be careful, get them to perform a test edit so you can examine their skill level yourself and feel confident that your money is being well-invested.

If you feel that this is not an area you wish to engage with, then it is strongly recommended that now is the time you research self-publishing companies in your area, which can take care of this work for you. As someone who works in this industry, I can tell you that you need to feel totally confident that you can trust the company and person you will be working with. You need to feel confident there will be an established relationship throughout all stages of publishing. Don't just go with the bare minimum or the cheapest. The investment you make now has to be carefully designed so you can see how it will be returned. The company you choose to work with needs to understand that and offer the information needed to give you this confidence. Later on, we take a look at a Financial Forecast Calculation example that helps establish expenditure vs. target sales vs. profit margin so there are clear and realistic measures of success and goals. To give you a rough estimate, and based on our 80,000 word novel that we mentioned during the appraisal process, realistically you should look between $1800 - $2000 for a structural edit.

Once you have selected a self-publishing company, they will contract and work directly with the editors, designers, printers, and promoters and report back to you.

Copy editing

Copy editing involves checking for inconsistencies in style, basic typos, and grammatical and spelling errors. With non-fiction especially and even most fiction nowadays, it is wise to check details. It is often the case that authors have made mistakes that many readers would not miss. Every author is different. Some authors are happy for editors and proof readers to make large-scale changes to their manuscripts – some are reluctant to grant quite minor alterations.

Quite often, structural and copy edits are done at the same time by the same editor and in some cases, proofreading as well. However, common practice is to have at least two people involved in this process. Remember to never edit and proof your work and believe it is ready for publishing. This is what too many authors do and it is guaranteed there will be errors.

Just quickly, let's take a look at expected fees for copy editing. Again using our 80,000 word novel you should expect fees of $1200 – 1400.

Proofreading

Proofreading is very similar to copy editing. Many manuscripts are proofread twice – once before they are laid out when all the text is completed, and again after the layout is complete. Again, *Track Changes* is very useful at this stage.

Proofreading also involves the final look over the entire document with the intention of eliminating any mistake in the surface features of the text or graphics of a publication.

Errors of accuracy in the structure or the text are the domain of the proof-reader in the final read-through after layout. But so are errors arising from the layout and pre-press functions because sometimes the design process can cause hiccups.

Don't settle for just anyone who says they'll do it. They must be capable. Now again, looking at costs for our 80,000 novel, expect to pay between $800 and $1000 for a quality proofread.

The following are general rules you should follow when preparing your manuscript for submission to most editors and proof-readers, and also for the design process. Ignore the traditional publishing techniques. Remember, you are making things easier and more economical to achieve your goal.

1. Type in single line spacing.

2. After a full stop at the end of a sentence, only one space is required before the next sentence begins.

3. If you are supplying images, then the files of an image must have a file name the same as it will be referred to in your text.

4. Choose your dictionary based on the country for which the book is most appropriate (if it is for international audiences, then US dictionaries are acceptable), then use the spelling and grammar checker on your computer to check your whole document. Look for the little red and green lines in Microsoft Word – right click and a suggested alternative will be offered.

5. Use the *Find and Replace* tool to find all possible problems in your manuscript and check them.

6. Find all quotation marks – first all the doubles, then all the singles, and check that they are they used in the right places and are consistent.

7. Find all italics; are they correctly used?

8. Find all common homonym errors that don't get seen by spelling checkers and check: there, their, they're, to, too, two, here, hear, your, you're, etc.

Order of elements

The pages in a book also need to be presented in the right order before the layout artist receives the work. Below is the common order of such material for the placement of pages throughout the book, though of course some books, fiction specifically, will only need a few of these.

Book half title - Imprint page (Copyright information) – Title page – Biographical Notes ('About the Author') – Dedication – Contents - Illustrations and Tables (list of) – Foreword – Preface – Acknowledgements – Introduction – Chapter 1 *(continue chapters)* – Acknowledgements (if not in the beginning) – Appendixes – and then if the following are required; Abbreviations – Notes – Glossary – Bibliography or References – Contributors – Illustration Credits – Index(es) (if necessary).

THE WORD:

Make life easy for your editors and proofreaders. Do basic spelling and grammar checks first. Have friends read it and review their feedback.

NEVER feel that because you have edited and/or proofread your own work that it is ready for publishing. You are far too close and things will be missed.

COVER DESIGN

We have all heard it, but it is complete rubbish: 'Don't judge a book by its cover!'. Of course we do. In publishing terms, a good cover is a major part of the marketing platform. It is what will encourage a potential customer to pick up your book. It should be designed to draw people to it. Once it is in your customer's hands, then the next thing they do is read the back cover blurb. This has to be well-written, concise, and enticing.

If your work is fiction, then the blurb needs to be captivating and should pose questions in the customer's mind that they are intrigued to find answers to. They must believe that by purchasing your book, they will receive these. If it is non-fiction the blurb should highlight the key selling points of the book. Establish with the customer what they will benefit and learn from this book, why it will be of essential education and learning, and how it will help inform and offer fresh perspectives on the topic.

I have mentioned this previously and will continue to enforce this: if you are not an expert in your field, don't attempt to be. If you are not a designer or graphic artist, it is not wise to design your own cover. Not only will it scream 'amateurish', but it will potentially turn your customers away. Your book cover has to pop.

My advice here is to outline or sketch ideas you have in mind for the cover, and then get feedback from your peer group much like I recommended in the writing stages. See how your friends, family, and colleagues respond to the ideas. Hopefully, there will be a consensus or even a merging of a few concepts to make the ideal design. At this point, you want to embark on contracting a cover designer to bring the idea to life.

Contracting a designer needs to be a well thought out process and my first recommendation is that you explore the avenues available through self-publishing companies in your area. By now, you should have made contact with a company that you feel comfortable working with. A company that listens and has a representative you can trust. Established and successful self-publishing companies usually have an in-house designer that can be contracted to design a trade standard and captivating cover for you.

Before you sign up with anyone, make sure you have seen samples of their work. You need to not only have confidence in the company that is assisting you but in the designers and other contractors working on your book. By viewing other covers and the explanation for the design, you should be able to ascertain if the designer has the creative and practical skills to bring the first visual impression of your book to life.

The cover is probably one of the key areas that independent or self-published authors fall down on. If what you have produced doesn't look great on the outside, then people are going to be less likely to take a look inside.

Keep in mind the people that you want your book to appeal to. What kind of image would draw in the right readers? I encourage you to be creative and original, but be mindful of your customers and remember that if someone is looking for an erotic romance, there is a certain type of cover that will attract their attention. Teddy bears and windmills don't sell erotic fiction. If you find yourself lost in coming up with ideas for your cover and want to give some guidance to your designer, try websites like bigstock.com as a source for imagery. There are also others like fotolia.com, Getty Images, BigStock, ShutterStock abstractinfluence.com, dreamstime.com, and many more.

With non-fiction, it is easier to be more defined in the concept. For example, a family history would logically have images of the family, the crest, or a prominent family member as the feature image on the front cover. My recommendation is to give a series of images to the designer and leave him to work his magic. Experience has showed me that the best designers work with flexibility. Trust them; they know what they're doing.

A good designer should take your concepts and ideas and develop several previews for you to review. I often expect three to be produced, often showing the same design but variations of it. In some cases, you can expect three totally different designs. Your job is then to get feedback. Ask your focus group that earlier commented on your writing to give their thoughts. Does the cover resonate with the story or writing? Does it stand out? Is it professional? Would they pick it up if they saw it in a bookshop? Evaluate what elements from the previews you may want to merge together or adapt. Who knows? The designer could get it right first time.

Always make sure the blurb has been thoroughly proofread as it has been known for typos to slip by on covers. You cannot expect your designer to proofread and they may make a typo or two. Through the support of the publishing consultant or publishing liaison, you should be able to receive a secure guarantee that they will take care of the cover editing as part of the design fee. Either way, have others review it also.

Key elements that should feature on any cover are the title, author's name, feature image (if the text does not stand in its place), back cover blurb, ISBN, and barcode. On the spine should be the title and author. Other elements you could optionally include are your brand or logo, or the logo of the company assisting you through the process. If you like, even the price and QR code can feature here. If you are unsure of any of these, then follow the guidance of your publishing consultant .

Once you are close to locking down a design, and if you have previously had a manuscript appraisal, hopefully you built a good relationship with the appraiser and you could send them a copy of the design in its entirety to see if it fits within the expectations they suggest for your book.

In conclusion, your cover needs to have impact. Research and see what other authors in your genre have done. If you are planning on writing a series and establishing your name as a certain type of writer, then build a brand. For example, all of China Mieville's covers show his name prominently and in mysterious font in the top third of the cover. The imagery has very abstract and contemporary design elements. It is the same on every book China publishes.

Some of the best covers I have seen to date are the most simple. Here is a list of some of the all-time best covers for you to review: The Bell Jar by Sylvia Plath, The Cat in the Hat by Dr Seuss, Jurassic Park by Michael Crichton, The Godfather by Mario Puzo, The Hobbit by J.R.R Tolkien, 1984 by George Orwell, and Psycho by Robert Block. Of course, this is my humble opinion. Personally, my favourite cover design from this list is Psycho. With the title running vertically and broken, it offers a haunting and unstable story. The title being so dominant infers that the 'psycho' character holds such prominence, at least to him. My favourite cover of all time envelopes the book you are holding. This should be the same for you - take pride in your <u>own</u> cover once you have finalised it. It will be the beginning of your brand.

We need to look at what you can expect to invest in a book cover design. Depending on who you work with and the elements of your design this can vary quite a lot. A standard, yet professional design using stock images shouldn't set you back more than $300, however if you have something more elobarate in mind like a photo shoot or illustration, costs can roll into the thousands.

THE WORD:

Don't judge a book by its cover? Of course we do so make sure yours has impact.

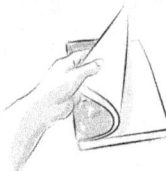

Before choosing a designer, request samples and ensure you are contracting an experienced <u>book cover</u> designer.

Always get feedback before locking down the final design. Ensure your cover is as good as the content.

BOOK FORMATTING

You should now have your book cover completed, or in the process of completion. Now it is time to focus on formatting your book to a trade standard. I know I am just like the record that keeps skipping, but I'll say again: if you have never designed a book before, don't start now! Hire the experts who do it for a living. Like the cover, there are certain styles and creative additions that help bring the best out of a book. Remember that your focus has been to write this work and an author who aspires to see their work reach great heights needs to enlist the help of a company that offers all the key ingredients to this journey.

Most of us can pick up the average novel and see the text is all laid out on the page the same way throughout the book. This might even create the thought that it can't be too hard to replicate. However, there are so many things to take into account, such as expected margin allowances, indenting, line spacing, drop caps, quotes and references, footnotes, chapter headings, and page numbers. All of these have certain trade style guides that publishers follow so readers can peruse easily though a book without confusion or complications. If your book includes images, then there is no choice but to enlist the assistance of an experienced designer who has formatted books. Photos, illustrations, graphs, and tables all need to be carefully examined and approved before placing in a book.

There are implications to quality if the images are not high resolution and copyright free, or are poor quality or in incorrect colour mode. A designer will address all of these aspects for you.

Again, ask to see examples of work the designer has done so your confidence is strong. Most independent or self-publishing companies should be asking the question: 'Is there any specific style or font or design element you want explored in this process?' My expectation would be that you receive a description form to complete, highlighting the key elements you wish to implement. This can include font choice, font size, drop caps, paragraph styling and more. If you are unsure, talk to your liaison and ask for guidance.

To give you a general idea of how standard text is approached by a designer, the font size is generally no smaller than 9 and no larger than 12. 12pt is considered a good reading font, especially if the book is a novel or around the average size of a novel. By size, I mean physical dimensions. Most novels can vary in size from 127mm x 203mm to 152mm x 228mm. A larger sized book may need a larger font, but typically, 12-14pt is the largest size you should ever use for any book. Most formatted books need to have the text justified both with width and height and a line spacing of 1/2pt to no larger than 2pt.

A serif font such as Times New Roman with a 10pt size is a good standard font to use as it is easy to read and pleasant on the eye. Sans serif fonts can also be used for body text - Arial and Helvetica are two such fonts. The page numbers should be in the same font as the main text in the book, and can be a size or two smaller than the main body text.

Chapter headings can be in the same font that is used for the body text, but for visual interest, a unique and larger font should be used. There should always be a clear two-line space between the chapter heading and the body text and quite often, this space is duplicated between the top margin and the chapter heading. A larger drop cap can be added to the first letter of the first paragraph to add visual appeal and emphasise the start of the new chapter.

An index is only used for non-fiction and in the new age of publishing is actually a rare element. It is usually set in two columns, with a space between them and the font size is generally one to two sizes smaller than the body text. Text in an index is also left justified.

A note at the bottom of a page is called a footnote. There is a lot to be read about the standard way in which footnotes should be formatted. You would be wise to look at how they are done in other books and perhaps refer to a style manual to review. The font size is generally a lot smaller.

As mentioned earlier, there is an order of pages expected in a book. When formatting is being completed, the designer will correctly place and design the book's half title, imprint page (copyright information), full title page, any biographical notes (e.g., About the Author), dedication, contents page, list of illustrations and tables, foreword, preface, acknowledgements, introduction, and every chapter that follows. If the book is non-fiction and it is required, the designer will also correctly lay the appendices, abbreviations, notes, glossary, bibliography or references, contributors, illustration credits and index(es).

The imprint page typically starts with a standard copyright statement like the following:

All rights reserved. No part of this publication may be reproduced, stored in a retrieval system, or transmitted in any form or by any means, electronic, mechanical, photocopying, recording or otherwise, without the prior written permission of the author.

If the work is a piece of fiction the following can also be included:

This book is a work of fiction. Names, characters, places, and incidents either are products of the author's imagination or are used fictitiously. Any resemblance to actual persons, living or dead, events, or locales is entirely coincidental.

The imprint page also contains information about where the book is printed, which edition it is, and the ISBN number, CiP and any reference to a website, blog, or contact to the author.

Photos

Authors aren't expected to know the specifications required when preparing photos for their book. In the case of photo art books, it is even more imperative that the processing of the images is correct so that when printed, they come out in the best quality possible. All photos need to be 300dpi (dots per inch) at a minimum. This qualifies the photo to be classed as high resolution and will therefore reproduce with clarity. If the photos are black and white, they need to be converted to greyscale. Often images appear black and white but are in fact sepia tone. On some cases, this is the desired result but if it is not or it doesn't matter either way, then greyscale them all. With the colour photos, they all need to be converted to CMYK colour mode.

There are several pieces of software that can assist with manipulating photos. None are better than Adobe Photoshop, which even for the beginner user, can be easily used to assess and adjust the colour modes, contrast and tones. Obviously, if as you read this it appears to all be foreign, it is another example of why you need to pass this part of the publishing process over to the experts.

Illustrations

With hand-drawn illustrations, the theory is the same. The resolution of the digital images needs to be at 300dpi minimum and the colour mode needs to be set correctly so the vibrancy of the illustration isn't compromised.

If the book you're producing is a children's book or a picture book, then this stage is vital as it is the illustrations that tell the majority of the story. It is important to seek advice from your consultant as to how best to have the illustrations produced for the book size you are looking at. For example, if you have a children's book that is 210mm x 210mm and you wish to have in the centre a double page spread, try not to have a vital part of the illustration drawn in the centre of this drawing. When it is placed into a design file, it may lose some impact as it falls into the binding of the book.

Also, if you wish the illustration to go to the edge of the page, then you need to create what is called 'bleed'. This is an additional 3-10mm of the illustration around each edge that can afford to be trimmed off, leaving the main focus of the image to be clearly seen.

With both photos and illustrations, they will obviously need to be scanned into the computer as a digital file. Your scanner should come with software built in that can be used for setting the scanning parameters. If not, Adobe Photoshop is fantastic and there is also free online software that can be of assistance. The main specification to remember is that you need to scan at 300dpi, colour mode must be set to what you require and of course, you must ensure that your scanner is clean. If you are scanning black and white images, then it would pay to increase your resolution size to 1200dpi. Ideally, you want to provide the designer with high resolution TIFF files, but JPEGs are acceptable also. Of course, if this is all foreign to you, supply your publishing consultant or designer with the original photos and let them take care of it.

Previews

Another important aspect of book formatting is reviewing the design file. Ideally, a good independent or self-publishing company will design the preamble pages and the first chapter for you to review and approve before they get stuck into the rest. Usually, the preview is provided in PDF form and here you want to examine the general look and style of the design. Again, get your focus group involved and allow for feedback. Compare the layout with a published book and give feedback to your consultant to review and implement.

Make sure the decisions you make here are definitive because changing your mind half way through the design process or at the end can be very costly. Several times I have witnessed authors confidently define a book size or font only to change their mind at the end stages of design, causing a delay in the process and additional costs. Take your time. Mull it over. Remember, you control this process, so make the best out of the preview and ensure you are comfortable with the style choices the designer has made.

Once the full design is completed, request the full book in PDF form to review. At this stage, you should be preparing a list of any typos, incorrect placement of text, images, captions, style changes, image replacements, or anything else that will affect the final design of the book. Once you have submitted your list, changes have been made and you have reviewed a new PDF file, you will need to give approval to the consultant that the file is complete and designed to your satisfaction.

Looking at our novel of 80,000 words, costs shouldn't exceed $1000 to format to trade standard. For children's books of say 36pages a professional book designer will charge around $500 – 600 and if you have a book that has images scattered throughout allow at least $10 per page for ones involving images and $2-3 per page for text. This is a great moment. You are now over a third of the way through this exciting journey and you can now step into the printing realm.

THE WORD:

If you are not confident in preparing the formatting and design of your book, seek the help of an experienced designer.

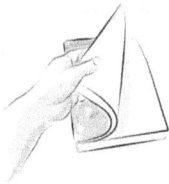

Always review the PDF file before locking it down. Check, check and check again.

PRINTING

When exploring your printing options, you need to be well-informed and well-guided. As I have consistently repeated, it is strongly advised that you contract the services of a self-publishing company you can trust to assist you in publishing your work. There is no more vital a time to do this than in anticipation for the printing stage.

The printing of your book can often be one of the largest monetary investments made during this journey, so it is essential that you have done your due diligence and researched which option is best for you. To help make that decision, consider the following: who is your market? How will you be promoting the book? Will you hold a physical book launch? Does it have international appeal? In a sentence, have you prepared a staged marketing campaign? With this, you can easily determine the need to hold stock of your book and if so, an estimated amount of copies you may need.

The marketability of the publication and potential audience has such a large influence on the printing methods used. For example, if you are producing a family history publication that you are planning on making available at a reunion, then you have already determined your market to be family and friends.

Take into account any potential interest from a local bookshop and/or library and you can approximately estimate the number of books you could sell. When considering your target audience, you can also determine if there is a need for an eBook or print-on-demand option of your work.

Print-On-Demand

Print-on-demand (POD) is a popular alternative in the new age of publishing, but before we explain when it is best used, let's explore what it actually means. The process is defined by the ability to print and bind one copy of any one book with ease, quality and economic viability. There are production differences between the POD products, a book produced through a digital high level production machine and a book that is created through the offset printing process. However, some selected POD providers can produce trade standard books to the same quality as expected through the traditional offset print-and-bind method.

POD is beneficial for so many reasons. The most obvious is to keep expenses low. If you can't afford a print run of some quantity, then a POD alternative offers minimal investment and the ability to meet a market with ease. The preferred POD providers are linked with international selling channels such as Amazon, Barnes & Noble, and Ingram. I will talk more about preferred providers shortly.

There does need to be some administration and design work done to effectively action a POD option and this is why working with the experts throughout is highly recommended as they can do the leg work for you at a reasonable rate.

The production costs with POD are the highest per unit cost from all the printing options available. This should be no surprise when you take into account the ability to effectively print one or two copies of your book and make it available for sale without having to hold any stock.

Also related to cost saving, if you're living in a country that has high postage costs, how can you be expected to provide physical copies of your book to an overseas market when the cost of postage is often as much as the book? POD solves that problem if you are tied to a preferred provider that has the POD system located in several major international countries. For example, imagine this: you have printed 250 copies for your reunion locally and halfway around the world, your favourite cousin said they couldn't make it but would love a copy. Rather than either of you having to foot the high postage cost, a preferred international POD provider can print in a location close to your cousin and save both of you a fortune with the click of a button.

If your book has strong international marketability, the POD module is a saviour. Ideally, you want to be connected with a provider that offers the ability for you to login to an account and see how sales are going, how profits are recorded, and when royalties will be paid. Without the POD module, your only alternative is to find a distributor who will more than likely want around 70% of the retail price for every copy sold and it will be your money that has to be invested into the production and shipping of the books to the distributor.

This is a risk that traditional publishers make and it is a big one every time.

Out of the thousands of books released each year, only a very small percentage cross over to the second run stage. The majority end up being remaindered for a fraction of the original sale price. Why take the risk? Why give away your profits to a distributor? These are all easily answered questions when self-publishing, and the answer is 'DON'T'. There is no need to take that risk when POD offers none and a much more realistic profit margin.

Now back to the preferred providers. When I first began writing this book, I told myself I wouldn't endorse any one company. I felt that the self-publishing journey was one to discover and educate yourself in. Then it dawned on me, you have done that by buying this book. So, it is now my job to continue ushering you down the correct path. In the case of POD, then, my recommendation is CreateSpace.

CreateSpace is an affiliate company of Amazon and offers the most comprehensive POD service ever needed. With CreateSpace, you can economically offer your book to the masses and have it all be managed from one online account. There are terms and conditions as with every POD provider, so it is encouraged to explore these to. At the very least, be informed. To use CreateSpace effectively, you do need to have relatively competent design skills so as to provide your files within their specifications. You will also be required to increase your administration knowledge as it is recommended to review terms and conditions, accounting information, and royalty calculations. The company you are working with should be able to take care of the implementation of this module and get it fully functional for you.

There are limitations with CreateSpace, such as paper stock, sizes, and binding, but you will find these limitations will be with all POD providers. Hardcover, saddle-stitched, spiral-bound or books with high photographic quality paper cannot be produced through CreateSpace, or any of the other major POD companies.

Like with any printing process chosen, you should always check a proof copy. With CreateSpace, you can choose to order a physical book to review, which does have costs associated with it, or you can approve an electronic proof through your CreateSpace account. The choice is yours, but it is essential that this process is completed and not ignored. It is the last step before your book is made available to the world.

Another essential piece of information you need to know is that once your royalty payment reaches $100USD, GBP or EURO, Amazon will either deposit your payment into a bank account located within the US, UK, or Europe or send a cheque to your postal address. If a cheque is the option chosen, I strongly recommend researching which financial organisation will cash the cheque with minimal fees attached.

More information about CreateSpace, specifically tax requirements, can be found on their website createspace.com. Make sure you take a good look and discuss this POD option with your publishing consultant. In my opinion, any book that you feel has an international opportunity for sales needs to be available through an international POD module.

Digital Printing

Digital printing is the next stage in printing following print-on-demand. While the technology is similar, the differences lie in capability. There are digital production machines specifically built to handle high run book printing projects in both colour and B&W, along with machinery specifically made to bind and trim small quantities of books. These machines have more flexibility with card and paper stock used. With digital production machines come low volume book binders. In a nutshell, digital production is the technological middle ground between traditional printing methods and 'coffee-machine' style one-off print and bind machines.

With some books, such as high quality children's books, coffee table books, or workbooks, POD is not an option and producing thousands is not economic or viable. Therefore, digitally producing a run of 100, 200, or even 500 is the best option and with trusted providers, you can guarantee receiving a quality product suitable to be placed on a bookshop shelf at a reasonable price.

As mentioned in the POD chapter, a proof copy is essential regardless of printing method chosen. With digital printing, this is even more essential as the financial outlay, once made, cannot be recovered; if you haven't checked everything but you've given approval to print, only to discover a major error that makes the book not up to sale standard. I have seen this happen too many times and the best advice I can give here is to take your time, check everything twice, give the proof copy to a trusted colleague or friend and ask them to proof and check. Once they are finished, you should check it again. Be 100% confident that you have exactly what you want.

If you do need to make alterations, I recommend producing another physical proof. Keep repeating this process until you have the certainty to proceed with the print run. It just isn't worth the heartache to rush this process only to be taught a lesson that costs you financially and psychologically.

Digital printing allows you to meet a local and national audience directly and through a carefully prepared staged marketing campaign (which we will discuss later) you should be able to promote to selected retailers, focus groups, neighbourhoods, clubs, media, libraries, public groups and more all within an acceptable distance from your location.

Building knowledge of your book begins at home. Your friends and family are the best ones to start a promotional train moving and having books on hand is essential to do this. Digitally printing the books and throwing yourself into local promotion helps your book's popularity pick up speed. Once local exposure becomes quite high, then a national push can begin and being able to provide books in a heartbeat and reprint another run quickly and economically is the strongest advantage with digital printing.

When selecting your printer, again, trust the judgement of the experts. Most established and reputable self-publishing companies either have an in-house production department or they have preferred printers, and these relationships are based on the quality of the product produced. It is recommended to trust their judgement when organising the production of your book. You may pay an additional fee for this, but it is better to leave the file preparation and printing processes with the people that do it on a daily basis.

This is not an area you want to heavily involve yourself in unless you have taken the time to learn and understand the procedure.

From an economical point of view, digital printing is highly feasible when it comes to producing print runs of 50 to, in some cases, 1000. With most books that are heavy in colour, the break point is at 500. By break point, I mean the stage when printing through an offset process will be more economical than digital.

Prior to the introduction of digital production for books, there was no alternative in publishing other than for an author to print a minimum of 1000 books. In many cases, authors have been left with unsold copies of their books for years to come. The most memorable story I have is from an author who now uses a box of her books as a step into her house. I will never forget that and will always advise authors to base their print run on how many sales they can make directly. If they exceed the target, then great! That is the time to reprint or take the step into offset printing if needed.

In my opinion, digital printing is the most logical option for any new author and any author who has a conservative marketing approach. If your goal is local, national, and international, then merge your digital production process with your POD module and have both active. At this point, you can enjoy local success with a digital print run and also offer the book to an international market through POD.

Offset Printing

Offset Printing is the most common and traditional method for producing books. Over 40% of all print jobs are carried out using offset printing. For decades, it was the only way. Now, it is used less frequently and only when there are key reasons to do so. Any well-known author (i.e. J.K Rowling, Dan Brown, Stephen King) has their books produced through the offset method as it is more economical for the publishing houses to do so. This allows for a greater profit margin and because the author is already established, the publisher can confidently guarantee sales to be high enough to warrant large print runs.

With self-publishing, the reasoning to print using offset methods varies, but fundamentally, it is because there is confidence that the author can move a high number of copies. Other reasons are reflected by popularity of a digital print run, company requirements, or purely profit-driven reasons.

Offset presses are primarily of two types. *Sheet-fed Offset Printing Press* allows a process in which the printing is carried out on single sheets of paper as they are fed to the press one at a time. The other is *Web-fed Offset Printing Press,* where the printing is carried out on a single, continuous sheet of paper fed from a large roll. The sheet is then cut into individual sheets of the desired sizes.

Offset vs. Digital

Offset printing uses CMYK (aka Process or Full Colour) and Pantone spot colour (PMS). This process uses ink and plates to transfer an image onto paper. It produces high quality cost effective results for long print runs.

As with digital, a colour proof is generated from the approved file for the final OK by the author. However, this may not be happening on the precise paper stock that the production run will be on, so final colour matching is still made 'on press' as the job is run.

Digital printing can print both CMYK (C-Cyan, M-Magenta, Y-Yellow, K-Black) and RGB (Red, Green, Blue), although colour shifts may occur with RGB content. Short runs of any quantity less than 1000 copies are typical for digital printing. As a digital printer requires no printing plates, there is less time and expense involved in setting up a file to print. This means that a finished file can be proofed and final quantity run within a short time period. Proofs can be printed on the actual stock choice for accurate colour checking.

So which process should you choose? The differences between the two processes can decide how to print certain jobs. Price based on quantity required and available times are obviously key considerations, but as offset offers the ability to specify PMS colour, this may actually be the better choice to achieve the desired result. The final printed effect of solid areas of colour can also be an issue to consider as digital printing can appear less impressive than offset, especially within certain colour ranges.

Cost is another factor. If your budget is limited, you may only have one choice. Finally, your market should have a say in the decision. Ultimately, you want to discuss the decision with your publishing consultant so they can give you an informed opinion. It is rather difficult to develop costs for each of these as the quantity has a major role to play during the financial forecast calculation, so for our 80,000 word novel we will discuss this later.

THE WORD:

POD – one at a time; Digital – 50 to 500 copies; Offset – 500+.

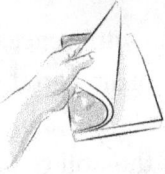

Prepare your marketing before deciding on your printing process and quantities.

eBOOKS

I t has taken a few years, but we can now confidently see that eBooks are a massive part of the publishing process and can have a profound effect on an author's success. Authors can now confidently release their eBook internationally and, with the use of online marketing techniques, open up their chances of creating very popular books with rewarding results. Before this technological development, an unknown author would never have had this opportunity.

Both authors and readers will always treasure hardcopy books, and particularly when publishing your first book, there is nothing like the feeling of holding your very first published book in your hands. However, publishing your book electronically as well as physically hugely widens the marketability of your book.

Having a published electronic version of your book means that you have a far greater audience, much larger promotional opportunities, and it strengthens your ability of making a greater return on your publishing investment. The eBook version is a stand-alone product that can be marketed differently than the hardcopy. It also requires its own ISBN number, unique from the paperback, so incorporate this into the process early on.

Customers can purchase and read it at the click of a button. If you are an established author, with one or a hundred books already behind you, now is the time to maximise your sales and publicity by releasing them as an eBook.

If you are a first time author, I recommend including this process in your publishing goals to increase both the diversity and the sales of your book. eBooks are now a critical part of the new age of publishing, and while printing hard copy books is still an essential part of the publishing journey, releasing your eBook meets the needs of a growing audience and will undoubtedly give you more selling opportunities.

So what is an eBook? The 'e' in eBook stands for 'electronic', as the book is a publication produced in digital form, consisting of text and/or images, and readable on computers or other electronic devices. Most can define an eBook as 'an electronic version of a printed book', but eBooks can and do exist without a printed version. In some cases, this is because of cost or for promotional reasons. Commercially produced and sold eBooks are usually intended to be read on dedicated eBook readers. However, computers and most mobile phones can also be used to read eBooks. Some eBook providers provide software that allows users to read their format on other platforms.

I believe all fiction titles should be published as eBooks along with generic non-fiction work, such as how-to manuals, self-help books, educational resources, autobiographies, and general history works. However, I don't feel that self-published authors should solely publish eBooks and in some cases, I have recommended against an eBook. There will always be a need and want for the printed book.

The eBook will never fully replace the printed title, but we can't ignore its presence and marketing abilities.

An eBook can be produced in different formats. PDF, Mobi, and HTML are some, but the definitive option as of 2013 is epub. Epub files can be easily adapted to all the currently available readers and are the most user-friendly files one activated. This means it opens up the selling and promotional opportunities available online. Most experienced IT or book design providers can produce an error free epub file ready for submission for sale with ease, but it takes time. It is desirable that they work with original files and create it from scratch. Many think that a suitable epub file can be converted straight from PDF, which is true to an extent, but the process can open itself up to errors with text and substandard image quality. It is best to again consult with the experts with this process.

I just want to step back for a moment and look at what kind of books should and shouldn't be considered for eBooks. Mainly due to my experience with some authors, I feel it is important to share this opinion. One of the best memories I have is of sitting on my grandmother's knee with her reading me my favourite books; the illustrations almost came alive with her enthusiastic animation. I will forever hold these memories close to my heart. This is part of why I believe that authors of children's books must produce physical copies, rather than living in the now and letting technology take over what we already know. Yes, it costs more to produce these books and yes, they generally take up more room than your average Kindle. However, how many children do you see carrying around an eBook reader?

This brings me to my next question: who buys children's books? Generally, it is not the child; it's their parent, grandparent, or a family friend. This reiterates the fact that the eBook should be looked at as an excellent addition to the physical book, not solely the only format available.

'How much should I charge for my book?' is one of the biggest questions facing the self-publishing author. The answer is: 'As much as you can'. Every author has the right to charge the highest price at which their books continue to sell consistently well. Lower than that, and you're doing your book a disservice. You might also be sending out the message that your book is not up to scratch and not worth the price on its cover. But you cannot overprice it either, as this could turn off prospective readers. It's nice to earn seven or eight dollars off each sale, but not if you're only making three or four sales a month.

You need to look around at your competitors to see what they're charging. Also, ask people what they think they should pay. But, if you're really serious about selling your eBook and getting paid what you're worth, then there's only one thing you should consider: how much is it worth? You need to approach the pricing by deciding that you're going to charge a reasonable value for what you're producing. And that value should be based on the unique factors that make up your product. People don't really buy on price. They buy on value, and then rationalize the price. If you have done a good job in promotion, then they should be almost convinced that the purchase is right for them.

Once price is set and your eBook is ready to go, you need to begin the process of distribution. This starts by ascertaining what are the most common websites that people buy eBooks. Amazon is the obvious one, but you also need to include iTunes, Barnes and Noble, Sony, Kobo, and Copia. These are the most popular sites that offer the biggest opportunities for sale. All take various commissions from a sale, so do your due diligence here and research, or alternatively, discuss this with your publishing consultant . Depending on the complexity of your book, prices to create and active your eBook channels will vary. However, for our novel of 80,000 words this should be somewhere between $300 - $400 to bring to life.

Finally, the only remaining discussion is the marketing of the eBook and the following pages outline how best to market both printed books and eBooks for the new generation. We are now on the home stretch. We are two-thirds of the way through our publishing journey; we have written the book, we have followed the strict process involved with the publishing process, and now you either have a print-on-demand version of your book, digital, or offset copies and/or an eBook available as well. Let's start promoting!

THE WORD:

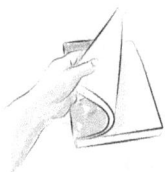

eBooks offer greater promotional opportunities for your hardcopy and in some cases can do even better

eBooks will never replace the physical, but you can't ignore it has a very important place in the publishing journey.

MARKETING

What is marketing? Marketing is the process of interesting potential customers in your products and/or services. As an independently published author, your customers will include readers, wholesalers – e.g., bookstores and specialty stores – anyone who buys the book from you at a discount and on-sells it, family and friends, publishers, literary agents.

It is essential to create awareness of your book for it to sell. Creating that awareness requires a focus of time and energy into activities that will increase your profile, the profile of your book and, most important, generate sales.

Considering your book as a product is part of the marketing process. For a product to sell, a customer must have confidence in the product or company. As an independent publisher, YOU are the company and the product is your book. Your customers need to know about you, your skills, your talents. Understand that while you are selling a book, you are also selling yourself as an author. Don't underestimate that value to a customer. A signed copy of a published book holds weight with the reader. While you have lived and breathed the work for months or years and taken it in stride, customers are excited to meet an author.

10 Towers of Triumph

Some self-publishers are born promoters and can confidently promote themselves and their work. For others, their published work complements their business or their area of expertise so they have an obvious and easy way to highlight and sell their work. For many, the content of the work is their passion or relates to a particular cause, so actively promoting it is something they are motivated to do because they want to share the content with others.

Other self-publishers are not so confident. However, acknowledging the fact that you, the author, are the best salesperson for your book is the key to your success. This doesn't mean you need to become a sales rep and hit the streets. Many of the ways to market and promote your book can be done at home, over the phone or via the Internet, and to your own groups of contacts – both personal and professional.

Now, would you believe this was one of the final parts of the book that I wrote? Sure was and the reason for it was that at the time the book was in editing, I had a meeting with a client about marketing. He had received their offset print run six weeks earlier and he was yet to implement any of his marketing campaign. His platform was set but there had been no progress and I was querying why he wanted to have another meeting about the marketing platform we had already created. We went over everything again before I asked the question: 'Why has nothing been done?' Nervously, the author looked at his wife and then back to me. He took a minute and told me he was afraid. It had become more real for him than ever and he had blocked himself from taking the first step into marketing.

I realised then that there needed to be a bridge between publishing and marketing that authors could cross in preparation for the next stage of the journey. I call these the Ten Towers of Triumph:

1. Personal Development – in a nutshell if we want things to change, then we need to change it. If we want our book to sell, then we need to sell it. As I have constantly repeated, there is no better sales person than the author – they have lived it, breathed it, and have the most passion for it. Once authors grasp this concept, they are on the way to eliminate the fear.

2. Total Well Being – your overall health – physically, emotionally, and even spiritually are connected. To successfully promote and market a product you believe in, then you should make sure the outside you is a good reflection of the inside you.

3. Relationships – we are who we are due to the relationships we have formed over our lifetime. In promoting books, you are also promoting yourself. Through the right mediums, build a relationship with your customer base. Have them like and trust you. Respect them and they will respect you. Money does not make the world go round, but relationships make the world go round because things get done through people.

4. Achieve your Goals – we talked about this earlier but you have to physically write down your goals – even the BHAGs. They manifest physically once you accept they exist. It becomes a reality.

5. Time - The proper use of time. Make sure you plan your campaign. Staged marketing campaigns enable you to achieve everything planned. Also, it makes you aware of the opportunities around you. Every day has many opportunities but usually only one best opportunity. The best opportunities are the ones that align with your goal.

6. Be a life time learner - Success can be learned through following the ones who achieved it. Whether it is attending seminars, videos, books, or other sources of information, it is important to learn what you can from the people who have already achieved this kind of success. Educate yourself. I know a lot about publishing and a little about everything else. If I don't know something, I Google it and learn. I won't be approaching the marketing of my book without learning from ones who have sold millions of copies of their own.

7. Life is sales - Sales means influence and influence is the key to a successful life. To have influence, you need to be perceived as a person with talent and virtues. You have the talent; you are creators. Virtues come with the belief in your creation.

8. Communication - It can be hard, but it is the key to everything. How and why we communicate is to achieve goals – mini goals and major ones. And, communication is also the skill of being able to actively listen. Listening to your customers is important. People don't care about how much you know until they know how much you care.

9. The world can always do with more good leaders. Through mastering the art of influence, showing interest in others and helping others builds trust and respect. Great leaders are real and they know who they are. They have an optimistic vision and they know how to work towards that vision. Be a good leader; be an expert in your art.

10. Finally, leave a legacy. Life is short. You can't choose how long you will live but you can choose how well you will

live. Your book is that legacy, so be proud to talk about it, promote it, market, and sell it.

If you spend time reflecting on the 10 Towers of Triumph, then you are setting up the change required to be a confident and successful promoter of your book. All you need now is the platform.

Setting Goals and Targets

All authors have a vision of success. This vision may have been the motivation behind writing and publishing your book. It is important to define your vision and goals, as this will assist you in your marketing and promotion. Success means different things to different people. Until you have defined what publishing success means to you, you really can't achieve it. So, it's time to ask, what does publishing success mean to you? What are the goals for your book? What do you want to achieve? You may want to consider your goals under three main headings: personal, financial, and professional.

Understanding your goals is the first step in setting your financial targets; the second step is to identify your market. When someone asks what your book is about, what they really want to know is, 'Why should I read your book?' As the author, you are, and always will be, the best person to sell and promote your book.

It was you who came up with the idea, put the energy and time into writing, had the passion to see it through to the publishing and print stage and now you need to continue that idea, energy, and passion into promoting the book successfully.

Don't be scared of any of this, it is just as exciting as writing or the publishing process and if you are unsure, talk to the experts. They will be able to help you in setting your goals, looking at investments, and what should be expected to make a return.

Here are some ideas to help you focus on what your goals could be:

- Personal
  o Develop my creative potential
  o Share my knowledge or story with the world
  o Entertain or educate readers
  o Become a recognised author
  o To have my books in libraries
  o People stop me in the street to talk about my work
- Financial
  o Recover the investment
  o Make a profit from my book sales
  o Take my family on a holiday from the sales profits
  o Make enough profit to fund my next book
- Professional
  o Be seen as an expert in my field
  o Increase my business opportunities through the book
  o Be asked to speak or present at seminars and conferences
  o Increase my profile and authority in a particular area
  o Use my book as a marketing tool for my business

It is important to follow your dream and to set the goals to get there. Write down what you see as your personal, financial, and professional goals and review them, asking yourself this question: are my goals realistic? If you feel that this is something that you may need advice with, ASK. You do not want to go into the marketing and promotion of your book not fully informed, without advice from the people who live and breathe books every day.

Spend some time thinking about your book and why people should read it. Try and sum this up in a 30-second pitch. Picture yourself in an elevator with a stranger and they have just asked you what you do. You tell them you're an author and have just published a book. They ask what it's about and you only have a few floors to tell them before they have to get off the elevator. Quick, concise and impact - that is the key. Once you get confident with the elevator pitch you should successfully be able to interest them enough that they enquire where they can get a copy. Make it clear, simple, and powerful. Now imagine this pitch as a 30-second book trailer where a viewer is tied to the screen and must be captivated by the visual and audio promotion of your book.

When marketing your book, you will be asked what your book is about, why you wrote it, what motivated you to write, and many other probing questions. You need to answer these questions with ease and confidence. You know why you wrote it; you must also consider why people should buy it and read it. In other words, what is the value of your book to the reader? What is your potential customer looking for? To position your book in the market you need to consider its key messages.

What is the purpose of your book?
- To entertain
- To tell a story

- To help others
- To share your experience
- To encourage and uplift

Statements like these will form the foundation of your marketing. Statements like, *'I want to be the next J.K Rowling'* will not really help you market your book. Hopefully, you will become the next big author, but you need to ask yourself whether this is something the reader really wants to hear. List the key messages in your book, how they are reflected in the book, and what the benefits are to the reader. Also, in conjunction with the benefits, what emotional response would you expect from a customer to these benefits? There may be other intangibles that your book offers its customers. For example, the ability to win or feel important, part of the crowd, or independent from it, environmentally responsible, charitable, etc.

Here are some examples to help you get started:

Educational/self help

> Key message: Healthy living
>
> Features: Book contains hints, exercise programs and diets; personal experience and success stories
>
> Key benefits: The reader will see how easy it is to live a healthy lifestyle, lose weight, stay motivated and feel great
>
> Emotional response: Relief, satisfaction
>
> Other; A solution to a problem

Fiction

> Key message: Vampires are merging with society

Features: Entertaining, challenging, riveting

Key benefits: The reader will be taken on a journey of intrigue and exploration, and challenged to suspend disbelief

Emotional response: Excitement

Other: Escape from reality for a while

Let's do it with your book

Key message _____

Features _____

Key benefits _____

Emotional response _____

Other _____

Independent publishing has created new opportunities for authors, providing affordable ways for you to publish your work and, with technology and out-of-the-box thinking, also opens up so many ways for authors to access new markets. There are many titles on the market and some may be similar to your book. Use this to your advantage. Take the time to consider what makes your work unique.

Remember when we talked about why the reader should buy your book? Another reason is — you. You make your book unique because, as an independent author, there is no better person to sell than YOU! Now, focus on what else sets your book apart from the others.

Visit your local library and bookstore, take a look at the books that are similar to yours, and ask yourself how your book is different. What sets it apart?

Creating your marketing budget is simple and built on the principle that you don't spend more than you can afford or wish to invest. Creating a marketing budget is not all about the money! Your marketing budget will include:

Time

Time is as critical an element of your marketing budget as it was when you were writing and working through the publishing process. In the world of independent publishing, you MUST put the time in to make the sales and meet your targets. Sometimes, this can get overwhelming and you don't want to burn out, so create a timetable that you can stick to where you allocate certain parts of your day to marketing and selling your book. This differs for everyone depending on the book and the goals set, but it is still important to allocate time to the project.

People

People are one of the most valuable tools in your marketing 'budget'. Gathering support from family, friends, work mates, social network forums, library groups, and book clubs is a great 'free' addition to your marketing efforts. Word-of-mouth recommendations and mentions on blog or websites need to be fostered.

Resources

This is about how you can use the resources at hand to market your book. For example, telephone, car, computer (Internet, email), business cards, flyers, and other printed support material. Consider how to incorporate these resources in your marketing plan.

Money

Many independent publishers fail to budget for marketing activities. Their investment in publishing their book has been the focus. You may have limited money to dedicate to a marketing budget, and that's OK. Marketing is achievable with little money, but in this case, you will need to be creative and prepared to commit sufficient time to it. The important thing is to ensure that what money you do spend is spent effectively and achieves results. For example, when going shopping or taking the kids to school, consider what else you could do to market your book on your way. In other words, try not to make extra trips in the car to market your book. Plan your timetable around activities you already do in order to keep costs down. Consider investing in business cards, flyers, and posters to assist your marketing. Do some research on the best options for you! Think outside the box. Always have one or more extra copies of your book in your car, bag, or workplace, as everyone is a potential buyer.

Choose carefully to whom you give free copies of your book and consider the follow-on effect of giving it away. Does the person or group have influence?

E.g. newspaper or magazine reviewer, book club, and whether they can write a review for you to feature on your website, blog, Facebook, etc. Some independent publishers choose not to give copies away, as they see it as a loss of income and a high cost. Others limit the number of free copies to give away as part of their marketing strategy so reviewers have an opportunity to review it publicly. Note that online reviews carry weight as well, and a protected PDF version of the book or eBook could work just as well and save you the out of pocket cost.

Your marketing goals may focus on how many books you want to sell over a period of time. You can work out how many that will be per month or week. Review the goal to ensure it is realistic. For many authors, moving into the marketing stage on their book can be daunting, so I recommend you create a staged marketing campaign where achievable goals can be ticked off one step at a time. For example, and keep in mind the following are very long term and loose goals:

- Print run 500 copies Printed 1st January
- Public Book Launch - target 100 copies Sold by 1st Feb
- Online Book Launch - target 75 copies Sold by 1st March
- Website/Video - target 50 copies Sold by 1st April
- Event marketing - target 100 copies Sold by 1st April
- Specialised Shops - target 50 copies Sold by 1st May
- Libraries - target 25 copies Sold by 1st June
- Bookshops - target 25 copies Sold by 1st June
- TOTAL SALES TARGET 425 copies Sold by 1st June

Now it's time for us to look at what exactly we can do to market and promote the published book so we can achieve these sales and beyond. In this new age of publishing, the traditional methods are secondary to what can be achieved online.

This doesn't devalue the efforts of physically promoting the book and those traditional methods still need to be included in the staged marketing campaign, but first, establishing your presence online needs to be achieved.

In the following chapters, we explore the key elements involved in building a staged marketing campaign and platform for your book. Remember, as the author and the person with the most passion for your work, you will always be the best salesperson, marketing decision maker, key promoter. A marketing campaign can be solely managed by you or a team of publicists and promotional staff, or you can discuss the strategy and necessary steps with your publishing consultant.

New Title Information Sheets

It is important that you designate a certain amount of promotional copies that you will use for soliciting reviews, gaining interest from retailers and distributors, and even giving away as part of a promotional tool. However, you want to keep this to a minimum and build interest for the book from samples and online tools. Even when you wish to wander over to the local independent bookstore to let the manager know you have published a book, you primarily need to present a New Title Information Sheet (NTI), rather than handing over the book.

An NTI sheet is a promotional document that details the title, author, publishing information (ISBN, Dimensions, Page Count), target market, price, author bio, synopsis, review, cover image, key selling points and of course, contact details, and point of sale. You can also have a review on this document. It is in a sense a condensed press release.

When approaching wholesalers, retailers and the media, an NTI sheet provides the key information they expect when being pitched a new publication. You may wish to provide a discount to wholesalers on the version sent to bookshops and libraries.

Obviously have a PDF version easily accessible both at home and even on your mobile device so this can be shown and shared at a moment's notice and I recommend having printed copies to leave with potential retailers.

THE WORD:

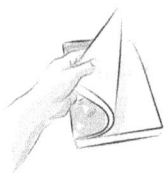

Make it easy for potential retailers of your book to make their decision. Give them what they expect.

Websites

As you have no doubt noticed, having a website for any product is an essential point of sale in today's marketplace. For authors, it is the platform of which your life as a writer is launched.

Whether it is focused directly on you as an author, a single publication, or a series of titles, we strongly recommend that this is addressed. Obviously, if your book has been published as part of a company tool, then the best option is to promote and sell the book through the company website.

A blog, if kept active, is an excellent tool to market to the masses. If your articles and entries are interesting, current, and informative, with the right focus, it can be an excellent launching pad for your publication. However, similar to social networking, only launch it from a blog if you know it will be maintained either by you or your publishing consultants.

The first decision you need to make is about your domain name. If you are creating a series of fiction books you could go with something like bobjonestrilogy.com, alternatively you could focus on the series itself and call it after the title of series title. If you are selling a book that defines you as an expert in your field then your name would be the best option. Whatever you decide, discuss it first with your publishing consultant as they will have good ideas based from their experience.

Try and keep the look and feel of your website neutral so that you can showcase your books without having the web design overpower it. Set the tone for you as a writer with your web design and think longevity. If you are writing or publishing many titles, then always promote the latest one with prominence. Make sure you have an enticing blurb with easy access to the purchase options. Include a link to read more about the book and even include an extract that people can download for free as a sample. If you have a great review or testimonial, include it.

People that hit your site will want to know about you, so include a professional headshot and a blurb about you that includes what led you to writing, and why you write the kinds of books that you do and what you love about it. Any interviews, blog mentions, reviews, or other media coverage items that occur can feature here or on a media page. The latest activity could be posted on your home page as it happens.

If your site has a blog, you can place an excerpt of the most recent post on the home page that is updated every time you publish. This keeps the content on your website fresh, and encourages people to explore the blog further and engage you.

Do I need to tell you how important social networking is? Not right now, I will later. For now just know that whether your preference is Twitter, Facebook, YouTube, Pinterest or Google+, you'll want to at least have a link to these pages so you're offering multiple ways for people to connect. Ideally having a Facebook or Twitter feed direct on your site will make it easier for others to connect with you.

Depending on the kinds of books you write, you might include photographs, video, or a series other things that tie into the content of your books. Sometimes authors are experts in their field and their books are an extension of a larger career — in this case, this is a great opportunity to include something interesting from the larger scope of your career.

A contact button is essential. It is your choice if you wish to publicise your direct email, phone number etc. but if you wish to keep your privacy, a 'contact form' can be designed so that enquires are privately sent to your email.

In order for your website to build traffic, meaning your potential readers, you'll have to learn how to market your website to the masses. While it is relatively easy to create a website nowadays, the hard part is getting people to come to your site. There are millions of websites out there on the internet, so no-one is going to just stumble on your site by accident. One of the most reliable ways to improve traffic is to achieve a high ranking on search engine return page. Let's go back to our science fiction novel website and because your site is so new, it's not even listed on any of the search engines yet, so your first step is to submit your site to search engines like Google and Yahoo. The pages on your sci-fi site include useful information about the book, exciting photographs, a biography on you and helpful links guiding visitors to purchase and possibly even other resources. Even with the best information about your novel online, your site may not make it to the top page of results on major search engines. When people search for the term 'sci-fi novels', they could end up going to inferior websites because yours isn't in the top results.

While most search engine companies try to keep their processes a secret, their criteria for high spots on these engines isn't a complete mystery. Search engines are successful only if they provide links to the best sites related to the user's search terms. If your site is the best science-fiction book website online, it benefits search engines to list the site high up on their pages. You just have to find a way to show search engines that your site belongs at the top of the list. That's where SEO (Search Engine Optimisation) comes in.

If someone went onto one of these search engine sites and typed in the words 'sci-fi novels' as a keyword, the idea is that search engines would display your website as a top choice. Naturally, people would therefore click on your site and be introduced to your book. However, it isn't that easy as you are not the only one with sci-fi books and using SEO, let alone the thousands out there cheating around SEO to ensure their website features at the top. This is where the assistance of your publishing consultant along with a dedicated and experienced web designer comes in. They help to define the keywords for SEO, ensure they feature regularly throughout your site so you have the best opportunities for hits onto the site. They should also manage the operation of the SEO and any other web campaign, such as AdWords.

We have covered some basics for your website and perhaps this might be new information for you and a skill base you don't have. If you have the skills, a website can be created relatively economically using template website designs. Domain names do have fees associated with them and need to be renewed usually on an annual or bi-annual basis as does the hosting company that holds your website. All of this is where working with a skilled web designer will help tremendously. If you have contracted a skill-assisted publishing service, then your publishing consultant should be able to offer this service or at least work with you in contracting a web designer. Again, don't step into this element alone. Contract the experts when needed.

Video Marketing

In this new age of technology, where we increasingly rely on multimedia to inform us of new products or services, it is recommended that you create videos to help in the promotion of your published work. The first is a video author interview. It should be no more than five minutes in length, and well-edited and filmed, as a bad production will distract the viewer and they will click away. You may be asking how this works and the best example I can give you is a personal story. I was never a fan of war movies and around 15 years ago, I randomly switched on an interview with Steven Spielberg prior to the release of *Saving Private Ryan*. I never knew he had family that were impacted by the Holocaust of World War II. I found the interview moving and looked at Spielberg in a different light. He had become more 'human' and this encouraged me to pay my entry fee and go to see *Saving Private Ryan*. I thoroughly enjoyed it and have since watched any movie made about World War II. An author will achieve a similar result. You will become a relatable entity to your potential customer. As a self-published author you are not only selling your book but also yourself as an author and this interview easily achieves this on a platform open to millions of people.

Customers who watch a video about any product will be more encouraged to buy. This is why television advertising has such a massive impact and it is also why authors need to begin developing their video promotional tools. Videos can be one of the best new ways to create the kind of buzz that attracts readers and sales. This new approach is part of the ongoing change in the industry's aggressive efforts to sell books.

As self-published authors, there is no denying that the old ways of marketing books has become prohibitively expensive and obsolete, especially in the current economy and declining retail sales in all sectors, so developing these innovative ways to promote and sell is only a good thing.

A 60 second video book trailer would also assist in heightening the book's profile and increasing sales. A book trailer is exactly like a movie trailer, produced to tease people into purchasing your book. This can be generated via still images, voice-over, stock footage, or even live action, depending on your budget. These videos are a great addition to your website and other online mediums such as Facebook, YouTube, Vimeo and more. Market your website and videos through your social networking profiles, email lists, author groups, YouTube, and other online video sites. Try and maximise exposure this way, as these are the most economical ways to reach the global audience. Don't attempt these videos by yourself, as a substandard product can actually do your promotional activity more harm than good. Again, hire the professionals and discuss these ideas with your publishing consultant.

THE WORD:

Remember you are selling yourself as an author along with the book. Promote both.

Always contract the professionals if you do not have the expertise to produce quality videos. Don't bring down the quality of the whole project by cheap options.

Social networking

Using social media with any success is a commitment. As with your book and the staged marketing campaign, building and maintaining updates, posts, and growing your community of followers is essential. This is a vital part of the national and international growth and success of the book. Don't underestimate it, but, don't be daunted if this is a new area for you, as it doesn't take long to learn and understand and it can be fun.

Social networking has become an everyday moment for millions of people worldwide. Whether it is a tweet, a post, a clip or a pic, everyone is sharing. It is also an excellent means for promoting books. For many authors, the journey into social media doesn't even exist until they start their marketing. Social media can play a huge role in promoting your book and also drive interested readers to your website to purchase. Not every social platform is going to work for every author and every audience, so what social media network should you start on? The answer to this depends a lot on the audience for your book. You have to know where it is they like to hang out. The list of social networking platforms grows all the time, so how do you know where to begin?

It starts with selecting the most well-known. The Fab Five are Facebook, Twitter, LinkedIn, Google+, and Pinterest.

Facebook is the medium on which you will find people you know: Friends, family, co-workers, school mates, etc. Because they know you, and want you to succeed, they will often 'Like', 'Comment', or 'Share' your posts, which means they reach their audiences as well.

Facebook is the most popular social networking site and it makes sense to have a page for you as an author or for your book.

Twitter is a place where people post in short bursts things they are experiencing or have recently experienced. They are posting how they feel, something that moved them, an inspirational story, how they perceive something, a funny video etc. If you feel you can tweet experiences that others would follow, then by all means, tweet away! Some types of tweets for authors to consider would be blogs, videos, events, and quotes.

LinkedIn is a site for connecting to other professionals. Some of the most successful self-publishers on LinkedIn are the authors whose target market are business people. However, there are authors who share all types of genres on LinkedIn. Again, think about your audience and if they would be a LinkedIn networker.

Google+ is fast becoming one of the largest social media sites because it's the place where you can truly connect with people you don't yet know, but who share your interests. It's easy to get started and add people to your circles, and connect with communities.

If you were promoting a cook book with unique Middle Eastern spices, it would be easy for you to connect with middle eastern food groups, cooking lovers, and other related communities.

Pinterest is a social media site for pinning photos into collections that are then shared to inspire others. It is dominated by young women. If you have images in your book that are compelling and inspirational, pin them and see if they drive traffic to your website, especially if your target audience is women.

It is essential that you start marketing using social media as soon as you can. Even when you are writing, start building online interest through these mediums. The key to social media is participation:

- Set-up an account to include a good avatar (should be your face, so people get to know you) and fill out your entire profile.
- Choose one or two platforms to begin with and build slowly so you know you are reaching the right target.
- Engage your followers BEFORE you market to them.
- Share, comment, tweet, like, and 1+ other's posts.
- Find articles that are related to you and post them.

Finally, if you are marketing using videos - video book trailers, video interviews, testimonials, chapter readings, book signing/speaking event highlight videos - don't forget about YouTube. It's not just a social media site; it's the world's second largest search engine. People are looking for you and your book there, and posting videos on YouTube can drive traffic to your website quickly.

THE WORD:

Connect with your readers through the obvious channels – social media. It is the place where you can find almost everyone!

Engage, Comment, Build, and Follow. Social media is about relationships.

Promotional material

From a local standpoint, building your profile is essential. When self-publishing it is important to start close and build out. This means that once your initial launch, on or offline, is over you need to build your profile in your local community. Posters, business cards and flyers placed at strategic places help build a fan base. For example, I frequent a local café here in the Gold Coast, I have become known to them and some other regular customers now get the 'hello nod and smile' when we are crossing paths for a latte. I have every intention on placing some small business cards on their counter. Who knows who will pick them up? I am confident that the frequent regulars and the staff will, but I could also come across, 1, 2, 10 or 100 people that have an interest in my book.

Your book's focus and target will determine what you should produce in support of building your profile. There is a range of items you could have, but I encourage you to discuss this with your publishing consultant as they would have more knowledge and expertise on what would be a good investment and what wouldn't.

For bare essentials, I encourage the production of business cards, 'with compliments' slips, posters, and invitations (if a physical book launch is planned). To help create a buzz, these items can extend to novelties such as bookmarks, postcards, fridge magnets, pens, flyers, rack cards, mouse pads, bumper stickers, and t-shirts! This is all dependent on your goal and budget.

If you are producing a flyer about your book, make it work for you by including an order form and return address so people can buy direct from you once they have your flyer in their hand. Always have your website and social networking icons on promotional material and be consistent as you are effectively creating a brand.

I recall, when working in New Zealand, an author I was working with replicated the front cover of the first book in his science-fiction/fantasy trilogy on both sides of his car covering the door panels and parts of both the front and rear guards. You couldn't miss it. He had a three line promo piece and his website. Driving to the local supermarket to get the groceries could have generated several sales. If your book is a brand or an extension of an established brand, this is an excellent idea. We all notice sign written vehicles and just like the cards at the coffee shop; you just don't know who will see it. The more, the better.

THE WORD:

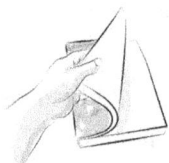

Build from the inside out. Start local and build your profile and your brand.

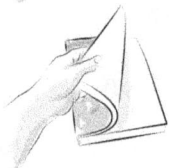

If you are proud of your book, be proud of yourself. Get out there and let people know you are an author.

Online Selling Channels

There is a multitude of online selling channels where you can promote and sell your work and all should be considered. Obviously the big ones like Amazon (see POD Printing), Google Books, Book Depository and Goodreads are all very effective when building a noticeable international presence and depending on your country of residence, these are likely to be considered essential. Make sure you research the distribution terms for each, as they will have varying percentages they will want for a sale, their fulfilment terms (meaning stock on hand) will also differ from each other.

There are then smaller websites that have international exposure which also need to be researched for their suitability. Again, this will be depending on book focus and market.

Take some time or request assistance from your publishing consultant to find the suitability of listing your books on websites such as Powells, Abe Books, Publisher's Weekly, Barnes and Noble, and Books-A-Million.

Once these and any other international online selling channels have been reviewed and activated, then look closer to home and search for the key selling sites in your country. For example, in Australia, Fishpond, TheNile, Wheelers, Red Hen, Seek Books, and Bookworld are the most accessible sites available. In most cases, listing your book on Nielsen's Book Data helps in populating many of these and more obscure websites with your listing. Each country has a different office for Nielsen's, so Google for your local contact. It is worth noting that some sites automatically populate their sites with your listings a few weeks after your ISBN registration is completed. I recommend regularly Google for your book and see if there are some listings as often they don't have accurate descriptions, covers or even prices. Contact them with the details they need to correctly feature your title. Recently a book about dating, which I helped bring to life was found on a website about the medical industry. Neither the author nor I have any idea how it got listed, but at the end of the day if it generates sales do we really care?

The next level of selling channels are the general sale and auction sites like eBay, TradeMe, Gumtree, Live Deal, Craigslist etc. A simple listing on a local auction site could build more profile than you originally thought, as once a product becomes popular, it becomes a noticed and in demand product. Plus the percentage you would pay to these auction sites is usually far less than what a bookshop would expect.

One very important part of Online Selling Channels is spreading the word. Once you have successfully had your publication listed on these sites, share the word. Through social media especially, tell your fan base the latest listings. It shows positive activity and popularity which again creates a mindset in the buyer it is worth a look.

Remember to consult the Financial Forecast Table when preparing to activate this option as discounts and percentages are a must for all of these outlets. The key here is to get as many online outlets as possible, as this can only increase your selling opportunities.

THE WORD:

The more online listings that feature your book, the higher the chance of a sale, so get on as many as possible.

Every new listing you find, share the word. It shows activity and popularity.

Book Launch (Offline)

Releasing your book to the public is so much more than that wonderful event where you deservedly celebrate your new publication with family, friends, and guests at a book launch and signing. Your off-line book launch should be both a celebration and a planned marketing event. You should set clear goals concerning how many books you want to sell on the night (part of achieving that target you have previously set). Ensure you have a team of three or four people to assist with some key duties. You need to ensure you have someone to take photos as these will be marketing tools for later promotion. Also, have a couple of dedicated sales people whose sole goal is to ensure every person, couple, or family have at least one copy of the book before leaving the event.

The Date

You may decide to have your launch coincide with a date of significance or event. For example, a romantic novel or a guide to relationships could be launched in conjunction with Valentine's Day.

Time and Day of the week

When thinking about what time to schedule your launch, you need to think about the people you want to invite and what time would suit them. Most book launches are held after normal business hours to capture working people. You need to think about whether to have it directly after work or later in the evening. Catching people on their way home from work may be better than asking them to come out after dinner.

The day of the week you select depends on the style of the book launch, the venue, and the target market, etc.

It may be best to launch a fishing book on a Saturday afternoon, but a family history on a Sunday. Think about what time of the week you would be most likely to attend a launch for your book's genre.

The Invitations

Send out invitations and ensure that the details of your book launch are clear, with the venue, address, and time included. If you are going to have entertainment or feature a celebrity speaker or giveaways, noting these details on the invitations will make the event more appealing. Indicate what payment methods you can accept. Invitations should be sent approximately three weeks in advance, and ask for an RSVP to assist with possible catering requirements. An RSVP will give you some indication of the number of people you can expect to attend. You may also wish to send out reminder cards/emails/texts to those people who have not yet responded.

Consider door prizes or entertainment to encourage people to attend – what you offer here depends on your budget and is an extra rather than something expected. Home baking or a few chocolates wrapped in cellophane is a simple, inexpensive and nice way to say, 'Thanks for coming'. If you do this, make sure you turn it into a marketing angle as well – include your business card in the packet with details of the book on the back and maybe a special offer.

Who should I invite?

Invite your family, friends, and colleagues. It is important to have people around at the event who make you feel comfortable and who will support you. Think about the market your book is targeting. Who do you know or could invite that fits this target market? For example, if your book is about birds, invite a local ornithologist to attend, or, if it is a fishing book, invite a local fishing club. Consider inviting the media, but be aware that they receive invitations to launches all the time and may not attend; however, be persistent and once an invite has been posted to any media representative, follow up with a phone call to confirm. Think about local business people, a celebrity in your area, or an expert in the genre or subject of your book. You may also invite them to speak at the launch. Here are some suggestions of people to invite:

- Local business people
- Local celebrity or expert
- Media
- Interest groups around your topic

- Service groups
- Librarians
- Book shop owners
- Family
- Friends
- Members of your local sport or social or hobby clubs
- Work colleagues
- Everyone and anyone you can think of who could attend.

Keep a detailed list of the people you have invited because the ones who didn't attend can be included later in your online book launch.

Book Launch Order of Events

Meet and greet people and thank them for coming. General mingling and introducing guests to each other is the key focus at this stage. Have someone monitoring any display or table you have set up, as people may be interested in buying copies early on.

Once the majority of people have arrived or you are now just a minute or two past the scheduled start time, have an MC or guest speaker publicly welcome everyone and give a brief speech about you, the author, and your book. This speech is the ice-breaker to get the ball rolling. How many guest speakers you have will determine the order they will speak.

One suggestion is that, once the MC has finished, the audience would welcome hearing from a close family member or colleague who has been supporting you in the publishing project in some way. This person will speak of how they have watched your dream unfold into reality.

The MC will thank the speaker and either introduce the next speaker (and so on) until you, the author, are welcomed onto the stage. This is your opportunity to thank everyone present for coming, everyone involved in the publishing of your work, and, most important, set up the selling of your book.

One possibility is to offer a discount if two or more copies are bought. For example: *"Self-Publishing Success – The Word' is retailing for $24.99 but for all who have attended today we have a special book launch price of $20.00, if you buy two — one for yourself and one for a friend, Christmas, or birthday gift — you may have two for $35.'* This is your book launch discount to encourage higher sales. End your speech by thanking everyone again and head straight to the signing table.

The MC will then quickly close off the formalities, welcome people to enjoy the refreshments provided, and to make their way to the book signing table to purchase their signed copies of the book. At this point, your team of sales reps get to work selling and handling the payment process, leaving you free to sign the books and talk to the buyers.

I recommended that you include a bookmark or business card when you sign each purchased copy as you never know whose hands it might end up in, which could generate another sale.

Stay at the table for as long as required. Following the final sale, mingle, relax, and celebrate. With the right planning and support, you should hopefully reach your sales target for the book launch.

THE WORD:

Have a team of committed sales people ready to sell copies for you. Make it a competition, eg. whoever sells the most wins a bottle of wine.

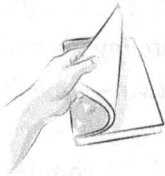

Encourage feedback. To your attendees, encourage them to email through their feedback. You can use this for more promotional activity.

Book launch (online)

Not everyone can attend your launch for various reasons or you may not be interested in having an offline launch. In my opinion, the people you would invite to a launch should, in theory, buy the book anyway so why spend more to have a party?

If you decide against an offline launch, then an Online Launch is a great alternative and if you decide to still have a celebration, then an online launch will be the next stage so you can capture a greater market of friends, family, and colleagues who can't make it to the party.

One way to do this is to create an Event on Facebook. Invite all your Facebook friends and leave the event open to the Facebook community outside your list of friends, as you never know who may attend. You may decide to go live and present your book to your online guests, share photos from the offline launch, pre-record video, or just open the chat. Make sure you have a clear image of the book cover, a solid description of the book, and maybe even a sample chapter. The focus needs to be on securing sales. This is easy enough to do by just offering them the same 'special launch price' or 'two books for $40' example offer before you release the book to the greater community. Also, to assist with locking in the sales, make sure you inform your guests that they will get a personally signed copy of the book – this is much more valuable to a customer than you might think.

The best method of payment is direct online bank deposit when holding an online book launch. Paypal and credit cards are options if you have the facility to process the orders.

A similar approach can be taken through other social networking sites, depending on the functionality of 'Invite to events' applications.

If you do not have an active social networking profile and you still wish to hold an online book launch, then a personalised email showing the book, photos, and the point-of-sale would be the next stage.

Time and Date

The beauty of operating an online book launch is the date and time can begin and end at your leisure.

It is recommended that you run the online launch for 24-48hrs, even a whole week if you can ensure you will maintain contact and responses. With Facebook launches, I recommend making a 48hours time period where your fans and followers can receive the special price.

Lead up to the book launch a few weeks before by creating an event and sending invites to your friends and networks. Have an image created using the cover, book information, special online launch price, and date.

Facebook Book Launch Order of Events

1. Once a date is set, create an online book launch invitation four weeks prior. Create a Facebook event. Post the invitation on your friends' and networks' walls.
2. Two weeks prior to the launch, send and post a reminder.
3. Day of launch. Post a welcome on your page to the official online book launch. Inform them of the posts that will be coming (samples, specials, free bookmarks, how to purchase).
4. Every three to four hours, create a new message you send to your friends and network. Structure the messages as follows:
   a. Back cover blurb, special price offer, and how to purchase.
   b. Introduction or preface, special price, and how to purchase.
   c. Testimonial, special price and how to purchase.
   d. First half of chapter one, special price and how to purchase.
   e. Book Trailer.
   f. Review or another testimonial, special price and how to purchase.

g. Second half of chapter one, special price and how to purchase.
h. Author Interview.
i. Announce end of launch at XX.XXpm/am so be in quick, special price and how to purchase.
j. Final post to purchase at special price.
k. Thanks and future order to be sent to email/Facebook/website.

Set yourself a target of 30% of the friends listed through Facebook to purchase. Following completion of the Facebook launch, implement a 12-week Facebook (and/or Twitter, Pinterest, etc) strategy that will continue the on-going promotion of your publication. Join and follow groups relative to your book topic and keep regularly connecting and sharing information about your book. Dedicate 15-30mins a day purely to social media promotion for the next three months.

Email

If you do not have an active social networking profile and you still wish to hold an online book launch, then a personal email campaign showing the book, photos, and the offer to purchase would suffice. The following outlines what is involved:

1. Draft a 'Welcome' launch email similar to as follows:
    Hi Jim,
    This email to you is one of a selected few I'm sending out to officially launch my new book 'Self-Publishing Success – The Word'. It has been an exciting journey writing this book and bringing it to life. I am so happy to finally see it

in print. I have attached the front cover, a link to my book trailer, and a brief overview on what it's about. (BLURB) I'm sure you will love reading it and I hope you'd like to purchase a copy. As a book launch special, you could buy a single copy for $24.99 or two for $40. You could buy one for yourself and one as a great birthday or Christmas gift to anyone you know looking at publishing. Get in touch if you would like to purchase some copies.

Looking forward to hearing from you.

Regards, Ocean

2. One week later, draft a second email and send to those who have not responded.

Hi Jim,

I have had a great response to my online book launch and copies are being posted out every day. I wanted to drop you another email as I hadn't heard back from you since I launched the book. I am about to take the book public in a couple of weeks where the price I am offering at the moment will be raised for the general public. So, here's your chance to get your copy at the special launch price of $20.00 or two for $35. Check out some of these reviews I have recently received and I have attached the introduction for you to have a read.

I look forward to hearing back from you.

Regards, Ocean

3. One week later, draft and send the final email.

Hi Jim,

Starting from next week, my book is going public, so this is your last chance to get a copy at the special launch price. Let me know if you would like to get your copy signed by me for $20.00 or two for $35. I can also sign one for a friend that you can use as a gift. Anyway, one more week to go Jim. Hope to hear from you soon.

Regards, Ocean

Mobile Phone

Finally, don't forget your mobile phone contacts. An SMS/TXT to your contact list with the same strategy I have previously mentioned will be just as effective.

Try to avoid sending group texts as you want to say their name so that the recipient can see you made the effort to approach them personally. Obviously, you have limited characters in a message so shorten your personal pitch so it will fit within one message.

Use the same principles as before by sending three messages over a period of time, but with this channel you can shorten the time in between each one. I recommend one message every two days.

You can choose to run a Facebook, email, and text campaign all at once, but whatever way you go, remember that the aim is to sell the initial run of copies as you would at a physical book launch, but without the cost of running one.

Keep a detailed spreadsheet showing your progress through each and always follow through as soon as possible. Once these contacts purchase and you have sent the book, you will want to follow them all up to see what they thought and if they would post a review on some of the major online selling channels featuring your book, mainly Amazon and Goodreads.

Include everyone in your email, phone, and Facebook lists when running the online book launch. Regardless of their connection to you - brother, father, colleague, old school friend - everyone is a potential customer and it is important that you get their support.

THE WORD:

Friends, Family and Colleagues. They are all potential customers. Don't be afraid to approach them as it is these people who begin your online popularity.

Commit to your Online Launch 100%. Follow up, respond and engage. You value these people as they would not be your contacts so value them as customers.

Soliciting Reviews and Testimonials

Reviews and testimonials are great marketing tools and they are inexpensive to get – you just have to ask. We suggest you ask your readers to write reviews of your book and then follow up with them on your request. The more people that say how much they enjoyed your book, the more likely you will achieve sales outside of your staged marketing campaign. You can post these reviews on your web page and social media sites, other online sales sites, on the back of your book when you reprint, and on any promotional material you print out or email. Reviews should be no more than a paragraph or two and should always state the reviewer's name and location. I also encourage you to request your reviewers to log into Amazon, Goodreads and other sites that list your book and post the review online. This is a massive part of your marketing as everyone looks at other readers' comments and it helps make the decision whether to buy or not.

Contacting the media to alert them of your book release is recommended. A successful interview or review will give the book added profile and generate sales. Try to find opportunities to be interviewed through local radio stations and newspapers. You will find community support is one of the greatest advantages you will have, so capitalise on it. As I mentioned before, with your staged marketing campaign, you build from the inside out. Start locally, then your greater state or territory, country and international. What you learn early with your local marketing will be invaluable when you reach international marketing.

Start with your local media; daily or weekly community newspapers, local community radio stations, and magazines are usually very interested in local human interest stories. Create a press release when you launch your book and send it to the media – in most cases your New Title Information sheet and introductory letter will suffice. Follow up with the local media by phone or email. You will need to be proactive as they receive a constant flow of calls and emails requesting interest in projects like this.

Over the years working for both traditional publishers and authors, I have learned the strategies that work and the ones that don't. Firstly, when contacting the media, don't expect a reply the first time. You must persevere. Make sure you research which media representatives you will contact. Find out who the person is and if you can, direct contact details. Once you have selected the media you feel is most appropriate to either review or feature the book, I recommend you send the New Title Information sheet to the media with an introductory email stating why this book stands out from the crowd. Try and keep the introductory email brief and to the point, remember that elevator pitch. The NTI is something they would be used to receiving when it comes to new publications being submitted, so you will already have a foot in the door.

Once you have made the initial contact with the selected media, the next step is to schedule a follow up phone call around 3-5 days later and ask if the email was received. This call is to reaffirm it has been sent to the right people. If possible, try and speak to the person responsible so you can make the following offer, but if you can't, ask the person you are speaking with to pass on the message.

Then state that you are prepared to offer up to 2 or 3 copies (definitely no more than 3) as free giveaways to their readers, viewers, and listeners if that would be acceptable. Finally, if you do not end up speaking to the 'shot caller', try and gather their email address for further communication.

The next stage is to immediately send an email thanking the liaison for their time and that you look forward to hearing back from them. Schedule a follow up email 7-10 days after this to see if there has been any decision made regarding your book featuring within the selected media. Try and include a useful piece of information that they wouldn't possibly know. For example, send a link to the Author Interview, Book Trailer, a testimonial, eBook release, and another review, or something else that will increase their interest.

The final step in this strategy is to call them 3 days following the latest email and make one last ditch effort to get a result. Usually by this stage, you should have a clear idea if they will be doing something with the book or not and you can either let the process take its natural course or cross them from the list.

This strategy has proven to be the most successful way of soliciting media activity towards self-published material. The only addition I would recommend to this is if the media is specialised. For example, if your book is about hunting, then when contacting a hunting magazine, call first and inform them that you are sending information through and basically you want to try and get the full information above through in one hit. These should be easily solicited as it fits their target market to review or feature a publication of this genre.

Many self or assisted publishing companies offer a Press Release Package where they contract a media distribution company to send the press release to selected media and then it is a wait and see process. This is a complete waste of time and money as these companies will send hundreds of releases on various products to the media on any given week and this makes it incredibly difficult for yours to stand out. This has to be the focus, what makes your book stand out? Why should the reviewers pick up your release ahead of someone else's? This needs to be answered because if you struggle with this, then how can you justify your customers buying. Talk to your publishing consultant about this and define those key selling points so it rolls off your tongue with ease. It is that elevator pitch that will leave the potential customer with a copy in their hands by the time they leave that elevator, remember that!

If your approach to the local media goes well, look for more opportunities on a larger scale, for example, suitable television opportunities. Again, make sure you stand out from the crowd and follow up your request. Don't simply expect them to call you. It may take several attempts over several months to get a response. Look for that angle. For example, if you are business speaker, you could approach a local business radio or television programme. Your success in promotion will depend on the content of your work and its appeal to a particular media sector, the way you approach the media, your passion, enthusiasm, experience, presentation of yourself and the information on your book, and on how well you communicate.

You will no doubt get some negative responses, but persevere – if you have a good product and believe in it, the positive responses will come. Some ideas which may help find suitable media contacts: Watch, listen, read!

Watch programmes that feature book reviews or authors. Note email addresses or contact details at the end of programmes so you can pitch your book to them. It is important to approach people who are promoting or appear to have an interest in the type of book you have written. Use the Internet. It's a great research tool where you will find contact names and phone numbers. However, be careful of 'mining' email addresses as you may breach anti-spam laws. Make sure you review your territory's laws on this issue.

Over the years, I have watched hundreds of authors follow this committed and focused strategy in soliciting reviews and achieving various successes from multiple radio interviews, newspaper articles, and magazine features. I have even seen a few television successes all brought on by self-publishers committed to their goals and the success of their book.

If your customers love your book, they will tell others, and this is where book sales really take off. This is the cheapest and one of the most effective ways of marketing; word of mouth. Ask people to tell other people because who better to promote the book than your readers? As I mentioned before, ask readers to email you their review or testimonial so it can be used on your promotional material, website, video, etc. Again, request that they post their review or testimonial on Amazon, Goodreads and other websites that feature your book and to make it easy for them, send the link to the sites featuring your book with the request.

Another way of building activity for the online listings of your book is to solicit online reviews. There are various websites, online magazines, blogs, and dedicated readers who make themselves available to review new books and they constantly publish their reviews online through various mediums, including social media and online selling channels. In some cases, you may have to pay for a review, but leave that option until last and make sure you include it in your marketing expenses so you can determine its possible gauge for return.

THE WORD:

The best form of marketing is word of mouth. Ask your buyers to spread the word.

When soliciting reviews, stay committed and follow through.

Event Marketing

If you are a business person or noted speaker, event marketing is an obvious way to sell your book. Whenever you run a training or information seminar or a speaking event, offer your book as part of the event, whether it is sold individually or as part of the seminar fee or even offer it at a discount for attendees. I quite often present free seminars on self-publishing and so often I regretted not having an add on book or product that I could sell to the attendees. Right there is a captive and direct group of consumers and whether it is 10, 100 or 1000 people they are your core customer base as they have an interest in your subject matter.

Look for trade show opportunities to profile yourself and your book. If you have the confidence and can see your knowledge and book topic as a presented product (e.g. a motivational self-help book), then think about organising a speaking event, or ask organisations, clubs, and societies who often have guest speakers if you can address them. It is a perfect way of getting your message out to a good number of people. Make the event free and focus on selling your book as the goal at the end. It may even turn into a regular business opportunity!

Craft fairs, car boot sales, street marketing, door to door selling, business events, market days, and other such community events are also a great opportunity to sell your book. Look for events like these occurring in your community and beyond, within reason and budget, in which you can participate. Talk about your events on your social media pages and website so people are aware you will be there promoting, signing, and selling copies of your book.

Most importantly, outside of these events, always have a copy or two of your book in your bag, car, office, etc., as you never know when an opportunity will present itself to make a sale.

THE WORD:

Especially if your book is non-fiction, look for any public events where you can attend and promote your book.

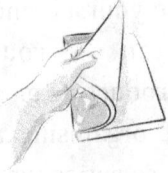

Always have a copy, or two, on you. Your bag, car, office – you never know when you will come across a potential customer.

Specialty Retail Stores

In this section, we will be looking specifically at bookshop marketing, but what I want to discuss here is that bookshop, library, and distributor marketing should not be looked at as the priority. With self-publishing, we have the choice to market directly and online prior to fitting into the traditional and less preferred option that many still see as the level of success. Do not limit yourself to bookstores and think hard about where your book may sell best.

The internet has put a squeeze on the traditional publishing methods. As you know, it is now much harder to get picked up by a publisher and to get your book stocked in bookstores. The only reason it will achieve that success is due to the publishing house and franchise stores seeing financial gain. The days of giving an author retail opportunities due to the content being topical or having a hook for the local community has become shorter. So, it is important to think outside the box when it comes to the retail opportunities. Consider specialty stores such as religious stores, fishing shops, museum shops, new age shops, gift shops, hardware, etc. For example, a local vet may be interested in taking your book if it is about training puppies. Once you have proven success locally, you can go wider. Another advantage of approaching specialty stores is that the discount or percentage they may take is often less than the 45 to 50% a bookseller will take, plus, you are actually reaching your market directly.

When I was a sales rep for a traditional publishing house in New Zealand many years ago, I had a children's book on my list that had a strong Christmas focus.

The book's release date was delayed which meant I had missed the key Christmas buying period from bookshops of early October. So, I had to think laterally and figure out an alternative so I didn't completely miss out on the key time period for Christmas buyers. So, I began asking the most obvious question a promoter asks: who is my market? As the book has a strong Christmas feel, it was logical to presume my first point of call would be retail outlets that also have a strong Christmas feel. So, I produced a database of Christmas tree and decoration outlets in my catchment area.

Then, I developed a larger list that covered the greater New Zealand. The approach was simple and effective and I will outline a generic approach shortly.

Once I had exhausted all the Christmas related outlets, which went relatively well, I evaluated the remaining stock and saw I was going to be left with a considerable amount of stock that couldn't really be moved for another 12 months. What could I do? It was back to asking some questions? This was a children's book. Who buys children's books? Primarily, mums! Mums are busy people, how do I reach them? Most have to take their kids to childcare and day care centres so that was my next mission. My timeframe didn't allow me to go much further than my immediate catchment area, which existed of 50,000 people, but I still managed to build a considerable database of centres and kindergartens. After a solid week of visiting, I had organised for every day care centre to take on ten copies and for every copy sold they received 25% for the centre. What didn't sell come Christmas holidays, I would pick up.

I had successfully sold more copies through the day care, kindergartens, and Christmas related stores in my small catchment area than in all the bookstores in New Zealand. Hundreds of books sold direct to the key demographic within only a few weeks.

I then began to introduce this form of marketing in other titles, with fantastic results. The best was a poetry book about hunting and fishing, which I successfully sold through boating, camping and fishing stores on a national level. All books have a market; it is just a case of establishing directly who they are.

There is a strategic process you want to follow when approaching the specialty retail stores. Firstly, print copies of your New Title Information (NTI) sheet which you should now have had produced. Also, save the PDF of the NTI on your computer so it is easy to access for emails. There are three database lists of specialty stores you should create: local, state/provincial and national.

If you are physically able, you could build a schedule for yourself to visit the local outlets in person. This offers more definitive and positive responses. When visiting the local stores use the sales technique below and make sure you take an NTI sheet and a copy of the book with you. Always ask to speak to the manager. Take copies of the book with you and have them in your car because if the store decides to go ahead you can give them stock, organise payment, and get things underway immediately. If you have a website, video, or online information that can help support their decision to say yes, see if they can go online to view so they are confident there is good promotion behind the book. The process in person is much like the online process but obviously adapted to suit face-to-face.

Email or present the NTI sheet to the contact email/manager from your database entries with the following pitch.

'Good morning _____, I'm touching base with you about the possibility of stocking my new book in your store. It is called _____ and is all about _____.

In this age of book publishing to be successful I have to look at how to reach the direct market for my book and it is logical to assume that stocking the book in a store where people have an interest in this topic will be more effective than a general book store.

I'm sure books aren't usually a product that you stock but, as I mentioned, the direct market will be your current client base so I see this working quite well.

What's in it for you? Well, my book sells for $_____ and I am prepared to give you a _% discount from this so you have the opportunity to make a good margin on each sale. I will also list on my promotional material (website, videos, Facebook etc) that my book is available from your store plus any interviews I do with the media I will also mention your store as a supporting outlet.

Attached is the New Title Information sheet so you can see what the book is about. I hope you find it enjoyable and something you'd like to give a go. I'm only seeking 5-10 copies to be taken on to start with and if successful I can send more when needed. I look forward to hearing from you.

    Kind regards _____ '

Now, from this initial contact, you may receive a straight NO. Fine, cross them off the list. You may get a straight YES. Great, next step is to find out how many copies they want and how they would like to pay. It is important that you first try for a no return sale so the store would pay up-front or on invoice and they own the purchased copies.

With the interested parties, keep a schedule to contact them in 3-4 weeks' time to see how they are selling so you can ensure that on-going sales are easily processed.

If they are not prepared to pay up front or on invoice, you could choose to offer a sale or return (SOR) policy where they take 5-10 copies and hold them for three months – your call. At the completion of the three months, you will need to contact the store and from the sales made, organise payment to be made (minus the discount percentage for the store) and send more if successful. However, a good retailer should be in touch when the book is sold out. Have a policy with your SOR agreement that any returned stock is returned at the retailer's expense and must arrive back in good condition for resale.

If, after the initial contact, you haven't heard anything within a week, then send the following email.

    'Hi _____,

I sent you an email last week about the possibility of stocking my book in your store. I thought I'd send you a bit more information to help you make a decision. Attached is a sample PDF of my book to give you a better idea.

Here is a link to my (website, author interview, book trailer, latest review, media activity, etc.). I hope you enjoy it and I look forward to hearing from you.

Kind regards _____ ,

If there is still no response from this contact, I recommend within a week you call them to see if you have been sending the email to the right person. If you get a firm NO, then cross them off the list. If you get a YES, then implement the procedure as above.

If you get an indifferent response, check the email address you have been sending information to and resend. Ideally, you should have a confirmed response after three points of contact.

This procedure is ideally suited to non-fiction books as finding outlets relative to the books topic is much easier.

THE WORD:

Think outside the box and market directly to the consumer. Whatever the topic of your non-fiction book, find retail outlets that already have a customer base of this genre.

Libraries and Bookshops

Most libraries and bookshops purchase through distributors, but if your book has a strong local angle, you are a well-regarded local writer, or if you think your book may be of value to the bookshop or library, you should approach them directly. Alternatively, find out who the local supplier/distributor is in your area and negotiate a percentage that works for both parties and, if agreed, they will sell your book to the retail outlets and libraries.

You must be prepared to give 40-45% discount direct to libraries and bookshops as this is what is expected and between 60-75% to distributors. Also expect that most bookshops operate under a sale or return arrangement of 3-6 months where if the books don't sell they will be returned and if sold, they pay at the end of the arrangements terms. Not ideal and that is why I recommend looking at this marketing approach at the end of your staged campaign.

The strategy in approaching libraries is very important. It is not easy to grab their attention and as you can imagine, they get approached regularly by authors and distributors. Before beginning this process I would like you to practice your 'elevator pitch'. Once you get confident with the elevator pitch you should successfully be able to interest them enough that they take a serious look at your publication.

So this is the approach to take;

1. Send the following email to the contacts in the library database (fill in the spaces with your information and any additional marketing information);

   'To Head Librarian,

   My name is _____ and I have recently had my book, _____ published. I feel this would be a welcome addition to your library and hope that you take a few moments out of your busy schedule to review the information I have attached. The book is retailing for $_____ and as expected I am offing a trade discount of

40% to libraries, bookshops and distributors. I feel it will have strong local and national appeal. Please let me know if you have any questions and if you would like to add this fresh new title to your shelves. I will call in a few days to ensure this email reached you and I look forward to your response.

Kind

Regards, _____

2. Three days later, call them and ask to speak to the head librarian or person responsible for purchases. Once you have them on the line ask if they received your email. If not, request their direct email and resend; ask when a good time will be to call back and discuss further. Talk about the book, and remember your elevator pitch.

3. If you have had to resend the information and have rescheduled a call back then great, follow through. If not and you have been told that they will be in touch, two weeks following this conversation, email them again with a friendly reminder and more information. Try something like this;

   'To Head Librarian,

   I have recently been in contact with you regarding my book, _____ and have yet to hear from your regarding the purchase of copies for your library. I just wanted to let you know that the book has been very well received and I have sold over ____ copies. I do not think it will be too long before I am sold out and wouldn't want you or your regular readers to miss out on a great new book by an Australian author. (THIS IS WHERE YOU ADD NEW INFORMATION SUCH AS VIDEO, MEDIA ACTIVITY, REVIEW, PRESS RELEASE, ANYTHING THEY DON'T KNOW ALREADY).

Remember that my book is retailing for $_____ and your library will receive the trade discount of 40% as expected. I look forward to hearing back.

Kind Regards, _____

If there is still no response after this then cross them off the list and move on. In some cases, libraries only purchase through a main branch library or a distributor. Ask who you should contact to discuss your book with them and make the call. As mentioned before, keep in mind distributors may ask for a higher percentage discount, they need a cut of the action as well.

This strategy has proven to be quite successful and has achieved with dedicated authors a 40% success rate from the reports I have had back. I personally know of one author who successfully stocked their book in over 60% of the libraries in Australia and had distributors take it on as well. So be confident, believe in your book and make a difference. Good luck and I hope to see your book in libraries soon.

With Bookshops the approach is much the same but there needs to be more creativity in your pitch and flexibility with your terms of agreement. First, remember bookshops are a business, they are there to make money and most aren't interested in glorifying a local author by taking on hundreds of copies to sell. However you can have some realistic expectations if your book is deemed suitable. By that I mean, a trade standard; professionally edited, designed and printed. If your publishing consultant gives you the green tick on those three aspects then you can feel confident that your book is trade standard.

95% of bookshops operate under for a Sale or Return (SOR) policy or on consignment, especially the franchises, and for those that missed my explanation of this, it is where the store will commit to stocking the book for 3-6 months and if sold, you get paid. If not, then the books are sent back. The problem I have with this is that over a 3-6 month period the books get picked up, browsed through, covers get creased, pages get dog eared and you can't really sell damaged stock. I strongly recommend that if you do have a bookstore prepared to take the book on SOR that you negotiate for them to take on 10 copies do a small display and have it on terms for 6-8 weeks. That way you have more chance of the book being seen and sold plus 6-8 weeks is more reasonable for the book to make an impact. This obviously increases your chances of sales plus if all 10 sell it will be more likely the bookshop will be in touch to order more. At this point you can renegotiate to take them on firm sale (pay on invoice).

40% is the minimum discount from the retail price expected by all booksellers and it is not even worth negotiating this. You have to expect them to want a clip on the ticket and it is the industry standard. In some cases, they ask for 50% and if this occurs then you have the ability to try and negotiate.

Always offer additional promotional value. Posters, bookmarks, business cards can be a valuable commodity in a bookshop as it helps draw attention to the buyer. The store may say no but if you don't ask... Also offer to do book signings and show that you are actively promoting your book though the media, social networking, direct marketing, whatever you are doing make sure to share the word with the booksellers.

Also mention to them that you will specifically promote that the book is available at their store through these same channels.

Much like libraries, most bookshops, again especially the franchises, will buy from a distributor but that doesn't make it impossible to still make it into store. Local bookshops are more likely to support a local author so make sure you print a copy of your NTI and wander down to discuss with the management. Keep a book handy but always show the NTI first. For those stores outside of travelling range I recommend implementing the same strategy used for the libraries, but obviously reword the relative text to suit.

Book signings are also a great promotional opportunity for both bookstores and libraries. I recommend making the time available and offer this to your local stores. Make sure you promote the signing through the earlier mentioned channels and a few posters in the area wouldn't go astray. Usually signings go for about an hour, maybe two, and they can often turn out to be more successful than you would think. A signed copy of any author's book is treasured by the buyer so don't write off the value of your signature. I recall being at a signing in Sydney a few years ago with an unknown author who had written about his time in the Australian military. Yes, he did coincide the signing with the week that Anzac Day was happening which made a difference, but before the signing we set a target of 30 – 40 sales max. He sold out of all the stock he brought into the store and I had to do a trip back to his car to pick up another box. In total 125 from 150 copies were sold in just over two hours. Also consider signings at events relative to your book. For example, at any writer's festivals occurring in my region this year, it makes sense I attend and promote my book. If you have written a book about the best fishing spots in your region and there is a fishing competition happening, get your rod and books and head down to the water ready to sign and sell.

The best piece of advice I can offer about promoting to bookstores and libraries is be positive, polite, prepared and patient. The P's again! Respect goes a long way in this business so make sure you show it from the youngest staff member to the seasoned and experienced manager to the elderly customer wanting a signed copy. Don't ever devalue the customer, even if they are acting as the middle man for your book.

THE WORD:

Expect to offer 40-50% discount from your retail price and bookshops to be sale or return/on consignment. But negotiate.

Book Distributors

Now we have reached the final point of call, the last step in marketing your book – the distributor. These are the dedicated teams of sale representatives who regularly visit the retailers and libraries to promote the latest titles they represent. The first thing you need to know is that distributors usually take 60-70% of the retail price. Forty percent is given to the retailer or library and they collect the rest for their work. This all makes sense and is fair, however not really for the author. Let's look at the book you are currently reading that retails for $24.99. With a distributor taking it on I would give away around $18 to the distributor leaving me $7 from each copy sold. Whew, I hope that covers my print costs, editing, design, ISBN registration, marketing and so on...highly unlikely.

So what is the plan here? Obviously the positive about a distributor taking on the book is selling bulk, however this will likely only be for a limited time unless you crack the market and that has to be the goal when signing with an dedicated distributor. However, for many self-published authors the marketing often won't support the distribution channel that will achieve high numbers sold. My recommendation is to generate so much interest with every other part of the staged marketing campaign that when you do decide to seek a distributor that not only could they have already heard of the book and are more likely to come on board but you could be feeling exhausted and quite happy to pass this responsibility on. Remember, you decide the life span of your book and if done correctly this can be indefinite depending on its popularity and how well-defined and successful the marketing efforts are.

Take a look at the best-selling book of all time, of which incidentally I bought the eBook last year, A Tale of Two Cities by Charles Dickens. Granted, the author is long gone, but the publisher continues to make money from sales of this classic which has surpassed 200 million sales. Too many? The Hobbit has sold 100 million and we can expect that to grow along with the Tolkien Estates royalty payments or how about something a little more recent, The Da Vinci Code has recently crossed over the 80 million mark and a personal favourite of mine and also self-published, The Celestine Prophecy has recorded over 23 million sales. Clearly it can be done and with the eBook generation gathering its momentum, it is even more possible to create a self-published best seller than ever.

Finally, there are main stream distributors that focus specifically on bookshops and libraries but there are also smaller companies that have more defined and boutique markets so do some research and look for a distributor that is best suited to your book.

THE WORD:

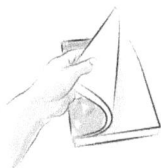

Expect to offer 60-70% discount from your retail price and make sure the calculations work out for you.

Financial Forecast Calculation

Before you can set a selling or recommended retail price (RRP), you need to consider the investment made to produce the publication along with the market to ensure that not only can you make your investment back but also that your book is well priced with its competition. The costs of self-publishing are not sunk costs, they are an investment. It should be, at the very least, one of your financial goals to recoup that investment.

Every publishing project is different and every author has a different set of goals. You may have invested in any one of the following in order to write your book:

- Manuscript or Market Appraisal
- Editing and Proofreading
- Illustrations
- Cover and Contents Design
- Website development
- Video Promotion
- Marketing
- eBook
- Printing

Don't look at writing time as something for you to recover. This is the one element of publishing that virtually every author accepts can't have a dollar value attached to it. Make the list as comprehensive as possible to determine a final dollar amount.

What you think people should pay for your book may be very different to what the market will actually stand. Do some research on books of similar type, size and presentation and get a feel for a realistic price. Check in bookstores or do a search online. If you have had an appraisal, this will help. Make sure you consider the eBook price also, as this will be an important part of your marketing campaign. For now, set a working retail price purely based on what you think at this moment.

$ _____

We all love a discount, and so do your readers and buyers. It is important to understand how the discount changes your financial return and to set your discount at a level where you are still making money, at least for the first 12 months of promotion.

If you are selling directly to a customer, you will usually sell your book at the full RRP. Where this might change is if you wished to discount your book for a special event. For example, at your book launch, you may sell an individual copy for $30 but, if they buy two, you will sell each for $25 (two for $50). Allow for this 'special occasion pricing' in your budgets.

A wholesaler is anyone who will sell your book for you. This could be a traditional bookshop, an online bookshop, a library representative, a specialist shop, a pet shop, or a health shop, etc.

A wholesaler on-selling your book will require a discount on the RRP so that they can make some money when they sell it. As mentioned earlier, the discount will vary from 40-50%. But, this is not set into stone and for retail outlets outside of bookshops; you will have more negotiation power. I suggest you look at the impact of your tentative retail price using three levels of discounts: 30%, 40%, and 50%. Each level of discount will change your profit margin.

Based on the example to follow, a 40% discount on a book costing $19 to produce (this includes pre-printing costs) with a retail price of $30 would actually lose money. The retail price would need to be increased or the discount level decreased to ensure you at least break even. It is important that you think carefully about your retail price and calculate the impact of discounts BEFORE you begin to offer them. You will need to decide what level of discount you can afford to give (if any) and what discount will still yield you a reasonable return. It may be that you need to review your retail price or the number of books you print to make it work for you. The formula works like this:

Example:

Retail price – Discount % = Price to wholesaler

$30.00 – 50% = $15.00

Or $30.00 – 30% = $21.00

Then the following calculation applies.

Price to wholesaler - Production cost per book = your $ profit

$15.50 – $19.00 = -$3.50

$21.00 – $19.00 = $2.00

Note: These calculations do not take into consideration your country's tax reporting requirements. I suggest that you seek financial advice on GST, TAX etc.

To calculate returns on your investment, gather all the costs (including your print costs) and you should now be able to work out what the total book cost per unit will be, at what minimum retail price you should sell each book for, the impact of discounts on your return and always remember, as an independent publisher, you control your prices, decide on the discount, choose the best retail price for your book, and set your sales targets. Build a financial forecast calculation sheet to assist you in the financial planning for your book and its success. While your goal may not be to make high revenue from sales, at the very least it should be to make your investment back. An example of a financial forecast calculation is available for free download on my website www.oceanreeve.com

Once you have looked at all the factors in the pricing of your book, have another look at the working retail price you have set. Here you need to ask the questions:

- Does it cover your basic print cost?
- Is it realistic?
- Will people pay that amount for your book?
- Is it too cheap?
- Does it give you enough profit to be able to recoup your investment over a reasonable number of sales?
- If you want to be able to give discounts, does it allow sufficient profit to give wholesalers a discount they will be happy with?

Once you have worked through these questions, you can then lock down what your retail price will be. This is no longer a working price. You have decided that the RRP will be: $ _____

The potential to succeed with your publishing project is quite high, as long as you are committed to promoting, marketing, and selling your book. You have spent months, even years, developing the publication to this stage – there is no reason why your passion should end. By making sales and being committed to your own success as an author, you will only drive yourself harder and be even more likely to meet your targets as you plan.

Using a staged marketing campaign, imagine if you sold five books a day from the print run of 500 books and you chose not to sell at any discount. In less than 4 months, you would have achieved the following goals we mentioned earlier:

- Personal
  - Develop my creative potential. **ACHIEVED** -you have written and published your book.
  - Share my knowledge or story with the world. **ACHIEVED** - you sold 500 copies.
  - Entertain or educate readers. **ACHIEVED** - you sold 500 copies.
    Become a recognised author. **ACHIEVED** - you sold 500 copies.
- Financial
  - Recover the investment. **ACHIEVED** - you sold 500 copies and met your target.
  - Make a profit from my book sales. **ACHIEVED** - you made over $X

Keep going and sell another 500, or more. Once you do the calculations on a reprint, where the majority of your set-up costs such as editing and design etc doesn't exist, the profit level is much higher.

- Professional
  - Be seen as an expert in my field. **ACHIEVED** - you sold 500 copies.
  - Increase my business opportunities. **ACHIEVED** - you sold 500 copies.
  - Increase my profile. **ACHIEVED** - you sold 500 copies

Marketing will sustain the life of your book and is something that you keep on doing, you never stop! Your marketing message needs to be heard over and over again to influence people to make a purchase – repetition works. To achieve this, it's best to use multiple marketing channels. People will buy if they:

- Read about you and your book:
  o In newspapers
  o On blogs, social media and websites
- Hear about you and your book:
  o On radio
  o From others
- They receive:
  o Flyers
  o Promotional information
- They are invited to:
  o your website
  o social networking group
  o your book launch or signing

Keep the excitement and momentum going – the lifetime of your book is sustained by your passion and pride in your work.

THE WORD:

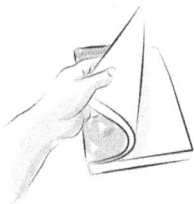

Sell, Sell, Sell. You have achieved success the minute you started this journey and every step that follows adds to this success. Selling confirms your success not only to yourself but also to the world!

Testimonial from Authors

Over the years in this industry I have met some fabulous people and I could write an entirely new book just on my experiences with authors. It has been a fantastic journey and I look forward to meeting many more in the years to come.

I welcome all new authors to get in contact and let's begin this journey together to self-publish with success. Defined, dedicated and determined. I would love to add you to the following list of happy and successful authors.

For that reason and also to share with you the successes that I have had working in this wonderful industry, and I suppose to also make a point that the information offered in this book can make a difference, I share the following testimonials from authors. Other than standard editing and proofreading, these have not been changed and are true statements.

I am humbled to have these authors feel so strongly about their experience working with me and as I have for them, they have all been such positive and enlightening additions to my life. While my chosen profession can appear to be quite - repetitive, author, book, publish, sell, - it is each author and their book that is unique, original and keeps this work very enjoyable and interesting for me. Without their tales, the good, bad and ugly, I would not be writing this book. So as much as this may have my name on the cover, this book is just as much a part of these authors as it is mine, and as it is yours.

'From every good story can become a great concept. From the first thought of a book idea to holding your finalised product in your hands for everyone & anyone to enjoy, Ocean Reeve made that possibility a reality. The novella, 'Worlds Away; Point of No Return', is owed to the professionalism no nonsense approach Ocean provided for myself as a first time author. The final product has been excellently received with the possibility of a trilogy definitely on the cards.'

Barry Kirkwood
'Worlds Away; Point Of No Return'

'I am a new author, which means I had no idea of what is required to successfully write and self-publish a book. However, from the first day I met with Ocean Reeve, working with him was a blessing.

He was available to answer my questions every step of the way; he gave me encouragement where I needed a push and told me everything I needed to know. Ocean is very approachable and he is amazing at his work.

All I can say is that I am glad I found him and feel blessed to have had Ocean work with and guide me through my dream of publishing my biography. I wish you all the very best Ocean, because the best of you is what you offer your clients.'

Memuna Barnes
'Survived; The Journey'

'My daughter and I are entering the final stages of being first-time self-publishers of a children's book, with the assistance of Ocean Reeve as our consultant and mentor.

As new voyagers on this exciting yet oft-treacherous sea of opportunity, it is a joy to speak of Ocean Reeve, because throughout the challenges entailed in self-publishing, it is he who has helped make this journey one of ongoing over-riding joys for us. From the moment Ocean's kind initial emails engendered the confidence within us to set sail and keep steering, his 'personable-ness' and expertise has been like a lighthouse. And I would hasten to add - a lighthouse with an obstetrician manning it – for I know (through the blessing of hindsight) that if we had tried to paddle our own canoe, it is much less likely that our book would have reached final stages of gestation.

My daughter and I have long been supporters of gentle natural birthing in our world, and Ocean is a gifted gentle natural birther in the publishing world.

I have so valued Ocean's 'style' of guidance, which is gentle, clear, and step by step. This has allowed us to fully focus on the particular task at hand at each stage of the process, while not being distracted or overwhelmed by too many of the complexities ahead. I have also valued the absence of any pressure re timing from Ocean, which has allowed this work to unfold and constellate itself naturally, in its own time. This 'zero pressure' is like the first part of an equation, the balance of which equals zero stress. With many other 'happenings' in life needing time and devotion (including the birth of beautiful children/grandchildren into the world) this absence of pressure and stress regarding publishing endeavours has been a wonderful saving grace, and deeply appreciated.

I'm also thankful to Ocean for his patience with those of us still 'learning the lingo' regarding publishing. He may have been tearing his hair out, there in his office – but we would never have known – for every time a dilemma arose, a quick email to Ocean would always be met by a prompt helpful response. Result: where we were stuck, we would be unstuck! (in the positive sense of 'unstuck'!) And appropriate perhaps to add that I seemed to find myself messaging Ocean the moment dilemmas arose – so sometimes at odd hours, or during a weekend, trusting he would find my message when next at work. Back would come an almost-instantaneous succinct, helpful answer.

So akin to the doctor with smartphone 'always on duty' image, the 'obstetrician in lighthouse' analogy lives! and begs a warm cartoon! (Abounding: gold plaques near door of lighthouse - letters after the name 'Ocean' designating degrees and honourary doctorates – in obstetrics, teaching, light-shining, self-publishing, etc. etc. ... and also abounding: weather-worn writers on rafts contentedly drifting ashore, ships of illustrators miraculously negotiating huge CMYK'd waves, and weary but happy self-publishers afloat in life-buoys – all following the steady beam Ocean is shining from atop his Lighthouse).

With that image, all that remains is to simply thank Ocean for being who he is; for his kindness, patience and personal warmth; for being inspiring and inspirational; for his teaching ability; for his vast expertise that he shares so readily, clearly, positively and freely; for being a gentle birther; for his

Lighthouse. I wish him every best wish for all his future endeavours, and commend him most highly as a consultant to anyone thinking of self-publishing. The world will be richer for your book being born, with its unique viewpoint and insights. So do it! Ocean is here!'

Betty Palm

'How The Moon Found Friends'

'Ocean has helped Cindy Rochstein Books grow amazingly over the past two years. The first work we did together was such an amazing investment for me, both financially and intellectually, as well as to the growth of my brand as it set the platform in which to launch the first of many successful self-published novels. Ocean's knowledge of the self-publishing industry was paramount in the way I chose to launch my books and his support throughout the entire process is without hesitation the element that sets him apart from others in his industry.

So far Ocean has helped bring three of my novels to publishing completion with ten more on the way. He understands that 'the devil is in the detail' and applies this to every aspect of the writing process from draft formulation, editing, graphic design, marketing strategies, press coverage and pitches to complementary industries, all to gain the exposure and sales that I require to increase the strength of my brand in this competitive industry.

I would never work with anyone other than Ocean and if you want success in the self-publishing world and implementation of your books into the world as well as company growth and brand development, where you know you will get the results- use Ocean. When a lot is riding on 'your dream' you have to be sure that the outcomes will be positive and I can't thank Ocean enough for assisting Cindy Rochstein Books in getting where we are today.'

Cindy Rochstein
'Women and their Stories'
'Mendemic'
'DATING...with children'

'I cannot recommend Ocean Reeve highly enough. From the onset his service was professional and efficient. Ocean was always with you every step of the way. His assistance with the creative was always on point and he was a pleasure to deal with on every occasion. I would certainly use his services again.'

Doriette McIvor-Stone (agent for Ian Hogg)
'You Wouldn't Read About It'

'Ocean is a highly focused individual, who, whatever the genre, believes in the authors he works with. He is also an approachable, reliable and knowledgeable anchor for the whole self-publishing process, and I look forward to working with him again. If only his book had been available when I started out on my journey!

Sandy Gent
'Wedding Day'

'In 2013 I made the decision to have my debut novel self-published. Where to start? I googled Self-publishers and, among others, Ocean came up. I contacted five of them, either via e-mail or phone. Taking the replies into consideration, I narrowed it down to two. It was not hard to choose Ocean to take care of my 'Baby'. Through his boundless energy, enthusiasm, knowledge, advice, encouragement and optimism, we soon had my finished product underway. Communication was first rate and it was not unusual to receive an e-mail from him at 6 AM or 10 PM, or even on a Sunday, such is his dedication to his craft. Readers of my novel have commented positively on the eye-catching front cover and also on the quality of the formatting and printing of the novel. I received good value for my money and would not hesitate to use Ocean for any future self-publishing I may undertake.'

Julie McCullough
'Of Wolves and Wildflowers'

'I am the publisher of several books and have worked with Ocean for several years. He talks to us on a level playing field and this to me is important. Ocean has the knowledge to give to self-publishers and I encourage anyone to ring him and talk with him their ideas. I have learned a lot and on my second book the proof reading module he implemented came out really good. Do ring him and talk over your dreams and ideas.'

Mitch Edwards
'Ending The Religious Lies'
'The Mind and Meditation'

'My first sailing book would have been scuttled long before it was launched if not for Ocean Reeve's expert guidance to navigate through the many reefs and hazards lying in wait just below the surface of the murky waters of self-publishing. Going it alone would have been like setting sail without a compass.'

Rob Oberg,

'Stuff it. Let's go sailing anyway!'

'My journey in self-publishing has been a great one but it has also been hard at times. Once I began consulting with Ocean Reeve things became a lot easier. Ocean showed true interest in my work, helping me through every step of the publishing process and really wanting my work to be shown in the greatest light.'

Simone Strydom

'The Hidden Land of Fairies'

'We found Ocean to be totally cooperative and supportive through the whole process. He gave clear and concise instructions when we needed guidance and we were delighted with the end product!'

Sharyn McKenzie

'Traditional Tales; A collection of stories from Burma and Africa'

'Ocean Reeve has a drive to succeed in the marketing and publishing world; not only for business but also for the clients who come to him. Ocean introduced me into the world of publishing and marketing when I approached him with my late Father's book to see if it was worth publishing. There are so many ways of publishing these days and he knows them all. His maxim is 'There is a book in everyone'. Ocean's reaction to my Father's book and his enthusiasm to guide me through publishing and marketing the book has brought a longtime vision into reality. He put me at ease and gave me so many avenues that I am now writing my own and making plans for a second. With this latest work by Ocean where he provides his wealth of knowledge on marketing, anyone can achieve their aspirations in the world of books.'

Linda Daniel
Editor/Author
'It Takes Owl Types'

'The knowledge of Ocean's experience in the publishing world has been invaluable in restoring my trust levels by his honest and refreshing personal approach. Ocean Reeve has a unique ability to identify each person's publishing requirements, tailoring his editors, front cover designers, and printing team accordingly.

After a terrible experience with another publisher, Ocean has helped clarify not just the basic steps involved in publishing but the entire process. He outlines the need to be active with my marketing and offers the support I always needed and wanted to make my self-publishing journey a success. I am delighted to personally recommend Ocean as a person who listens and genuinely cares about successful outcomes for my novels, in today's realistic marketing parameters.'

Carmel Joyce

'The Bosun's Quest for Fairer Skies'

'I took on an enormous task when I decided to self-publish my first book; a full-colour, high quality tutorial of 260 pages for professional photographers.

I was lucky to find the knowledgeable assistance of Ocean Reeve, who had the book beautifully printed and helped me then to market it. Both of these areas were a mystery to me when I began. Having Ocean's skilful contribution to complete my project, I can feel proud of my achievement as an author and look forward to rewarding sales.'

Russell Brown

'Paths to Artistic Imaging in Photoshop'

Ocean is dedicated to providing quality service to their clients. I have used him to organise the editing of my novel and its follow up book, and he managed to turn both of these into works of art. I will always recommend him.'

Luke Murphy

'A Compendium of Yesterworld'

'Being a first time editor revising my late mother's book, I have been delighted to have Ocean as my mentor. I was unfamiliar with formatting, book design and other publishing requirements and Ocean has kindly stepped in to impart his expertise.

As an insecure person, I tend to fret and Ocean has gone out of his way to reassure me. I cannot thank him enough. I appreciate the personal touch he brings, his unfailing availability, and his patience all of which have lifted my spirits when they were flagging and they have indeed helped build my confidence. I am very grateful for his support.

He was prepared to comply with any of my requests for changes when he deemed them necessary and gently advising me to the contrary when they were not .

He has an easy manner on the phone and I could actually see his smile shining through his emails.'

Marie Ternel

'Grammar for Beginners'

'Writing a book is all about communication. As an author you feel as if you are the one doing the communicating and everyone else has to read and, hopefully, enjoy what you put out there. But really there is much more to it and it is when the task comes to transform the manuscript over which you have slaved into the polished and marketable creation that so many authors come unstuck.

I thought I had got my manuscript to an almost ready-to-print stage. It was far more complex than I had believed and am so fortunate to have had Ocean on my side getting through the myriad of steps. Where I was getting frustrated with my own editing and proofing, Ocean appeared to become more patient. When the proofs were finally completed and approved he swung into action and obtained all the necessary data to make it all happen. He kept me informed all the while with print timings and marketing ploys and dates when the book would be available online and ensured the funds were flowing appropriately.

Ocean, I now count as a friend as well as my publisher and I thank him for walking the journey with me.'

Jay Lawry
'The Scenic Route to Paradise'

'My experience in dealing with Ocean throughout the process of having my first book published was excellent. Considering my poor computer skills Ocean walked me through each area necessary and no question was too difficult. Ocean always found a way to work with me on the areas I lacked. As a result my book was successfully published and has been selling well. Ocean has always endeavoured to answer any questions, even after the publication in October I am confident and am looking forward to working with Ocean in the future.

Lora Brand
'Beauty for Ashes'

'In the publishing of our book "Shailer Families The Daring Pioneers", we had issues with the quality of the pictures. Because some of the photos were such poor quality when they were sent to me and some were of good quality, we couldn't seem to get a quality printout. After five drafts and a lot of frustration on both sides mine and work from Ocean we finally got the best balance for the photos.

My thanks go to Ocean for helping me sort out the issues and to get the book to the printer just in time for the book launch. There were some anxious moments that we would not have any books to launch, fortunately we received most of the books at 6 pm the night before the book launch.

I have had a lot of positive comment to the quality of the book since the book launch. The cover of the book was designed through Ocean's designers and looks really professional. The advice throughout the process of publishing the book was extremely valuable and a huge learning experience for us.'

Beverley L Shailer and Deborah M Farrar
'Shailer Families The Daring Pioneers'

'When I started looking for help publishing my book I found Ocean Reeve. I thought it had to be fate as my children's book series is about Max, a boy learning to surf and his best friend Little Dude a dolphin, so I thought if his name is "Ocean" he must be meant to help me on my journey. So I made the phone call. I found Ocean to be very easy to talk to, he helped me every step of the way. From publishing, marketing, book trailer and Author Interview (and believe me, I was nervous).

Ocean made my self-publishing experience a dream come true. Now I have my first book published and available in eight bookstores as well as my website, Amazon as an e-book and surf shops. If you are looking for that down to earth, friendly and very professional person to help you with your publishing journey, then look no further Ocean is your man!'

Michelle Hennessey

'The Adventures of Max; Little Dude'

'After my first meeting with Ocean Reeve I knew we were going to do business together. I was impressed by the way he listened. This was Number One on my list. After reading my manuscript he asked questions about the plans I had in mind for my children's book.

Naturally as a first time author I have much to learn, in consultation with people like Ocean who are educated and experienced in the business. I feel I can trust Ocean to help guide me on my mission – and trust is the essential foundation for a good and lasting relationship.'

Fay Moxly

'Is Santa For Real'

'Over the past six months myself, Margot Stephens & Toni Behrens, two professional artists who teach part time have published a small, high quality book enabling many students to realise a dream of being published illustrators. As we had no prior experience in publishing this was a remarkable achievement only made possible by the support & guidance of Ocean Reeve. With the success of this first publication we hope to create a much more ambitious project this year with broader community involvement. We hope we can continue working with Ocean to bring this project to a successful launch later in the year. Thanks Ocean, your support has been invaluable.'

Margot Stephens & Toni Behrens
'Mother Goose Nursery Rhymes'

'In 2012 I finally made the decision to write and publish a book. I wanted to use an Australian business for the design, publishing and printing. After emailing various businesses, Ocean Reeve, responded instantly, answering all my questions. Not only did Ocean respond instantly, he was actually only one of three who did!

In those early days Ocean proved a source of amazing knowledge and continuous support. He guided me through every step of the publishing process. His response times are always extremely timely and he is always bending over backwards to help out throughout the whole process. Ocean is the only person I would trust to work with me through this process when I am ready to compile my next book. I cannot recommend him highly enough.'

Silva Mirovics
'Handbook for the Aussie Vegan'

'I can't speak highly enough about Ocean Reeve who has made publishing my book, totally 'pain free'. Ocean was able to help me produce a beautiful, top quality book, with colour illustrations throughout, exactly the way I wanted, in very quick time, which was important to me for family reasons.

Besides publishing the book, Ocean set up my Amazon online account, and gave me valuable marketing advice, and great service, in a friendly, professional manner.

I have no hesitation in recommending Ocean for any self-publishing need, and I will certainly be using their expertise to publish my future works.'

Wendy Campbell
'The Newmarch Quest'

'When the student is ready the teacher appears! I feel so blessed to have found Ocean and to work with him in collaboration on my latest projects. After self-publishing three titles with great passion however with little guidance, it has been such a pleasure to find Ocean with his wealth of experience and knowledge of the publishing industry. Ocean supported my dream of releasing my titles internationally and with ease and grace he gave my Angel books wings to fly worldwide via the eBook and Amazon POD platforms. Forever grateful!'

Michelle Newton
'Angel Altars'
'The Angel Feather Oracle Companion Book'

'The first step to self-publishing I took was with Ocean Reeve. He has been great in providing all the information I needed and led me down the path to become a successful self-published author.

Guided me all the way and respected my wishes. I gained so much courage that I self-published my second written work through them and getting ready to publish the next one. I value the efficiency, being on time and downright easy.'

Stefka Harp
'Heart & Soul'
'A Collection of My Father's Bedtime Stories'

'It seems very fitting that Ocean Reeve publishes his first book about self-publishing. The guidance and advice he has provided for us from the nerve racking first step, to the final product, has freed us of the worry and allowed us to focus on what we love, writing. When it comes to such a massive leap into an unknown world there is no other person we want in our corner. The success we have enjoyed from the early days of publishing our first novel that has now grown to a second and third can be contributed to Ocean.'

TNT CORLIS.
'The Keeper'
'I Do 2'
'The Bowers Mill'

"I found Ocean to be a great help in bringing my book from a raw product to one that impresses all who view it. He also gave me a lot of guidance and help in establishing a programme of marketing"

Colin McFarlane

'Travelling Australia by Road'

'I highly recommend Ocean for anyone wanting to fulfil their dream and self-publish a book. His hard work and dedication is testimony to his work ethic and professionalism.'

Justin Hasell

'Your Powerful Potential'

'Having spent fourteen years compiling my "Epic", which ended up being more than 660,00 words and 632 A4 pages of verse, I didn't even bother to send it to a traditional publisher. Having put all that work into it however, I was loathe to just put it away and forget about it so I approached Ocean with the view to self-publishing. He guided me through three proof copies and made suggestions as to the content (besides the basic text) of the finished publication. He organised the cover design, with which I am well pleased, and gave advice on many aspects of marketing. Every time I look at this hefty tome, I am delighted with the finished product and with its five-star review on Amazon as well as the many compliments from friends. I can do nothing else but recommend his services.'

Rex Callahan.

'The Best and Verse of the Twentieth Centruy'

'Ocean worked with me to publish a large and complex theological book of 718 Pages in Crown Quarto size. During this time I was most unwell, battling terminal cancer and palliative cancer treatments. Although there were difficult periods where I wondered whether I would live to see it completed, the project is now in its final stages and I am grateful for the way Ocean worked with me in getting my book 'across the line'.'

Ken Butcher
'The Church; What On Earth Is It?'

Final Note and Acknowledgements

A milestone has been reached. Thirteen years in this industry has not all been collaborated in this book and I am absolutely ecstatic that you have made it to this page. It means that you are now one step away from beginning your publishing journey. No doubt over the years to come I will continue to learn and grow in this industry as I hope you will too and I am sure to publish a second edition. We never stop learning and while I consider myself good at what I do, I develop and find new and innovative ways to make publishing an even more enjoyable experience every day. I strive for my authors to succeed as it is their success that I share in and helps build my own. Without it, this is just another self-publishing book. I hope you can see the defined, dedicated and determined way to self-publish and that you can succeed with the right approach and staged marketing campaign. Next I embark on fine tuning a process for self-publishers to economically produce audio books and I'm motivated and excited to begin this journey and then share it all with you in due course.

This book would not have been possible without the relationships I have formed over the years with others who work in the industry and of course the authors.

I wish to acknowledge every author I have worked with over the years. You have all contributed to this book in some form and for that I thank you.

I want to make specific mention to Ian Packman, author of *The Stones of Akron* trilogy. Ian has been just as much a teacher as a student and together we have helped each other grow and succeed.

Ann Kidd, author of *Mummy, You're A Dick*. Your humbling words and award nomination made me see something within myself I had yet to see. Your book has made a difference as I always knew it would, but most importantly, it gave you closure and I am grateful for being able to help bring this book to life.

Daniel Keighley, author of *Sweetwaters; the Untold Story*. This book was published traditionally and it was really through this I saw the true opportunity for self-published authors. This was one of the best books I have ever read, but the marketing never did it justice and this was no fault of the author or publisher. It just needed unique marketing approaches that are not implemented by publishing houses.

I also want to thank and acknowledge all the authors that have written testimonials for this book and my website. As I mentioned, I am humbled by all of your comments and will always treasure these. Thank you.

The acknowledgments to the people I have worked with in this industry could also be another entire book but I will try and make it short. First my editors, Kaya Ra, Jessica Seaborn and Linda Daniel, to my cover and web designer, Jai Johannessen and to the team at InHouse Print & Design, I thank you all.

Whilst many of the following people no longer work in publishing, they have all contributed to my knowledge in this industry and my ability to write this book. Without them, this book just wouldn't exist. For the desire that one day these people get to read this book, I would feel privileged that when they have reached these final pages, they see how grateful I am for their wisdom, respect, education, opportunity, faith and insight. So my special thanks to Graeme and Jane Beals, Allan and Raewyn Stonnell, Paula Reid, Andrew Ginever, Rochelle McDonnell, Jamie Shotter, Karen Watt, Julie Bromfield, Adrian Wright and David Longfield. You have all participated in bringing Ocean Reeve, self-publishing specialist to life.

Finally, my family; together we have grown with humility and have always tried our best to respect and value each other's opinions, goals and aspirations. It is these skills that I share with my authors on a daily basis and will continue to operate under. Listening is one of the greatest skills in the world and while it is not always practised to its full extent, I take pride in being able to listen to my authors and help them achieve their publishing goals and aspirations.

So that is it, The Word – self-publishing success defined, dedicated and determined. I hope you have enjoyed this book, learned from it and feel inspired by it. For further guidance and assistance, I am here when needed. Contact me through my website oceanreeve.com and I look forward to sharing in your self-publishing success.

Self-Publishing Success

- THE WORD -

Defined, Dedicated, Determined.